Designing Organizations for High Performance

Designing Organizations for High Performance

David P. Hanna
The Procter & Gamble Company

 Addison-Wesley Publishing Company
*Reading, Massachusetts • Menlo Park, California • New York
Don Mills, Ontario • Wokingham, England • Amsterdam • Bonn
Sydney • Singapore • Tokyo • Madrid • San Juan*

This book is in the Addison-Wesley Series on Organization Development. Editors: Edgar H. Schein, Richard Beckhard

Other titles in the series:

Organizational Transitions: Managing Complex Change, Second Edition
Richard Beckhard and Reuben Harris

Organization Development: A Normative View
W. Warner Burke

Team Building: Issues and Alternatives, Second Edition
William G. Dyer

The Technology Connection: Strategy and Change in the Information Age
Marc S. Gerstein

Power and Organization Development: Mobilizing Power to Implement Change
Larry E. Greiner and Virginia E. Schein

Stream Analysis: A Powerful Way to Diagnose and Manage Organizational Change
Jerry I. Porras

Process Consultation, Volume I: Its Role in Organization Development, Second Edition
Edgar H. Schein

Process Consultation, Volume II: Lessons for Managers and Consultants
Edgar H. Schein

Managing Conflict: Interpersonal Dialogue and Third-Party Roles, Second Edition
Richard E. Walton

Library of Congress Cataloging-in-Publication Data

Hanna, David P.
  Designing organizations for high performance / David P. Hanna.
      p.   cm.—(Addison-Wesley series on organization development)
  ISBN 0–201–12693–1
    1. Organizational effectiveness.   I. Title.   II. Series.
HD58.9.H36   1988
658.4′02—dc19   87–35502
                                                                         CIP

13 14 15 BAM 9796

In memory of John H. Feldmann, Jr. and C. Wayne Richards—
their High Performance Organizations are carrying on. . . .

Foreword

The Addison-Wesley Series on Organization Development originated in the late 1960s when a number of us recognized that the rapidly growing field of "OD" was not well understood or well defined. We also recognized that there was no one OD philosophy, and hence one could not at that time write a textbook on the theory and practice of OD, but one could make clear what various practitioners were doing under that label. So the original six books by Beckhard, Bennis, Blake and Mouton, Lawrence and Lorsch, Schein, and Walton launched what has since become a continuing enterprise. The essence of this enterprise was to let different authors speak for themselves instead of trying to summarize under one umbrella what was obviously a rapidly growing and highly diverse field.

By 1981 the series included nineteen titles, having added books by Beckhard and Harris, Cohen and Gadon, Davis, Dyer, Galbraith, Hackman and Oldham, Heenan and Perlmutter, Kotter, Lawler, Nadler, Roeber, Schein, and Steele. This proliferation reflected what had happened to the field of OD. It was growing by leaps and bounds, and it was expanding into all kinds of organizational areas and technologies of intervention. By this time many textbooks existed as well that tried to capture the core concepts of the field, but we felt that diversity and innovation were still the more salient aspects of OD today.

The present series is an attempt both to recapture some basics and to honor the growing diversity. So we have begun a series of revisions of some of the original books and have added a set of new authors or old authors with new content. Our hope is to capture the spirit of inquiry and innovation that has always been the hallmark of organization development and to launch with these books a new wave of insights into the forever tricky problem of how to change and improve organizations.

We are grateful that Addison-Wesley has chosen to continue the series and are also grateful to the many reviewers who have helped us and the authors in the preparation of the current series of books.

Cambridge, Massachusetts   Edgar H. Schein
New York, New York   Richard Beckhard

Preface

Why This Book?

In recent years there has been much written on becoming excellent or developing High Performance Organizations (HPOs). Generally, the books or articles that deal with these subjects provide valuable insights into the experiences of those who have achieved various levels of excellence. However, many of the managers I have worked with have been simultaneously inspired *and* frustrated by such materials and the numerous programs they have spawned.

"OK," one manager said to me a few years ago, "now I know what a High Performance Organization looks like. But how do I *develop* one?" His question has been repeated by many others with whom I have worked.

Alas, there is little written help available to answer such requests. Most of the literature on HPOs is either purely descriptive or primarily conceptual in nature. What the reader finds today are many documented situations of high performance or case examples in which one is invited to analyze the organization design elements (structure, work design, rewards, etc.) which were adjusted to produce superior results. There are also many valid comments on these design elements and how they are related to improving results.

Much of this information is necessary, but not sufficient, to produce high performance. To elaborate, these materials are necessary because they identify what one must *know* or *understand* in order to create HPOs. But they are not sufficient because they do not bring the would-be implementer any closer to actually *doing* anything to put the theory into practice. What they omit are the valuable insights into the processes that were used to translate organizational concepts into bottom-line improvements.

Filling the Gap

Filling the gap between theory and practice is my purpose for writing this book. I believe this undertaking is unique in two respects:

1. *Its Target Audience.* This book is written for those managers who would like to develop higher levels of performance in their organization, but aren't sure how to go about it. There are two types of managers who will benefit most from this book:
   a. The manager of a discrete business unit that can have an impact on results.
   b. The organization consultant who is looking for tools to help others manage the process of developing High Performance Organizations.

   In each case, I am assuming the reader is out to make a difference in his or her operation. That's what high performance is all about. Without a commitment to making a difference, the reader will find much of what is written here excessive and exhaustive. This subject is *not* one that can be handled quickly or easily.
2. *Its Approach.* My focus here is on how to implement various theories to get better results. This means I will not be comprehensive in my treatment of the relevant theories or concepts. Rather, I will address only the ba-

sic theoretical foundation one would normally need in order to manage the process of developing HPOs. I will use a how-to approach and share experiences concerning not only what others have done to intervene in their organizations, but also how they arrived at their plan and how it made a difference in results. Those who really want to develop high performance will be able to see the processes others have used successfully.

The how-tos will be concerned with two aspects of design:

a. *The rational part*, including identifying the desired organizational model, structuring the various design elements to produce the required results, and assessing one's progress at any point in time.

b. *The emotional part*, including educating members about organizational alternatives to the bureaucratic model, developing their commitment and support for the model actually chosen, changing habits and practices to fit with the "model system," maintaining commitment "when the going gets tough," and renewing the model when circumstances require it.

No Quick Fixes

Many managers, it's sad to say, delve into the subject of high performance without fully understanding the theory, principles, or the art of the process involved. They merely attempt, in piecemeal fashion, to copy some general techniques that are reported in the literature, such as work teams, visioning, or quality circles. Most often such attempts are disappointing. Frequently the unexpected and unwanted side effects produce results that are the opposite of those intended. Unfortunately, this is often the case when a quick fix is attempted on a complex organizational system.

Developing high performance is not a quick fix activity! High performance requires a lot of work. The whole work system must be conditioned if performance is to be high. Attempting to create high performance on a piecemeal basis is akin to training for a marathon race by exercising only one part of the body each day. It takes years to create a change in the entire system and additional years to refine and renew such efforts so that high performance is enduring and not just a flash in the pan.

Sounds pretty imposing, doesn't it? Don't despair.

Taking the Mystique Out of High Performance

As a young graduate student, I once sat in awe as one of my early Procter & Gamble mentors, Herb Stokes, worked with us to design a process for developing a High Performance Organization. Herb was outlining a process flow that would teach participants some basic organization design principles and then coach them on using the principles to actually redesign their own organization. "How do you do it?" I asked in amazement. "I wouldn't know where to begin with something like this."

"Oh, I've done it so many times, I hardly even think about the process any more," was Herb's reply.

Those who have experience in developing High Performance Organizations can help demystify the process for those going through it for the first time! This book is an attempt to "demystify the process" by consolidating many of the principles and practices that have emerged from those who have gone through them before. In the more than thirteen years that I have worked in the field of organization effectiveness, I have been fortunate to work with excellent colleagues in the Procter & Gamble Company and compare notes with many design experts in other organizations who have been gaining similar experience. Some of these organizations include AT&T's American Transtech, Cummins Engine, Digital Equipment, Donnelly Mirrors, Exxon, General Mills, Hewlett-Packard, IBM, Sherwin-Williams, and Signetics.

In comparing notes with these companies, it is apparent that the high performers aren't smarter than others. They aren't possessors of some magic model or formula. Most often, they have tried many times to create high performance and have only learned successful approaches through the years by trial and error. Each has evolved an approach that has worked for him or her.

Common Design Principles Override Most Differences

Though approaches certainly differ, designing and developing systems capable of high performance involve certain principles of human behavior that are truly universal. The issues are remarkably similar, no matter what the nature of the organization is, or the culture in which it operates. The examples in this book come from organizations as diverse as health care units, manufacturing plants, consumer goods marketers, engineering shops, religious organizations, and high tech industries. The basic framework and many of the approaches have been used with good success in all cases.

These common issues also transcend different geographical locations and foreign cultures. For example, when I first was assigned to work in Europe, I was struck by how consistent the experiences of high performers were regardless of whether they were in England's industrial belt, the Rhine valley in Germany, the lowlands of the Benelux, or in Italy. About this same time all of the literature on "Japan Inc." began to flood the market. Although many debated the suitability of Type A cultures versus Type Z and other models that tried to explain the Japanese phenomena, I came away with a quiet reassurance, recognizing that underneath all these academic debates were some principles of work design in top Japanese firms that were strikingly similar to what many of us in other settings were implementing.

A Cautionary Note

Having labored to convince the reader of all that is common for those pursuing high performance, let me now provide a caution. As will be seen in subsequent chapters, I do not espouse the philosophy that there is one best way to do anything. The danger is that what appears in this book will be viewed as a standard recipe for solutions to someone else's problem. This is certainly not my intent.

The principles described herein are truly universal; the specific techniques much less so. I advise the reader to focus continually on these principles and recognize the techniques only as applications that have worked for some individuals in their particular circumstances. Some of the techniques may be applicable to other situations as well. But any particular intervention that is chosen must be done with sensitivity for the current state of affairs in the organization. In other words, some customizing of tools, techniques, and approaches is a must. I have included as many examples as possible to encourage the reader that any organization can be transformed into one that is capable of high performance.

The Organization of This Book

Chapter 1 gives a review of the theoretical roots behind high performance technology. Open Systems Theory, an outgrowth of General Systems Theory, is presented as the most comprehensive model we currently have to replace the bureaucratic model, or Machine Theory of organization, which has been our model for more than two centuries. The implications of Open Systems Theory for managing HPOs are discussed.

Chapter 2 presents an overview of an Organization Performance Model that I have found to be particularly helpful in understanding how all of the pieces fit together when one wants to: (1) assess organizational effectiveness and (2) design systemic improvements in performance.

Chapters 3 and 4 discuss these two processes in greater depth and provide real life examples of how each has been used successfully in other organizations. The two major applications of Systems Theory, Open Systems Planning and Sociotechnical Systems design, also are outlined in Chapter 4. Some of the strengths and weaknesses of these past approaches are reviewed.

In Chapter 5, I elaborate on some techniques to approach some of the most difficult design issues: drawing departmental boundaries, team design, and designing work roles for individuals.

Managing Cultural Change is the subject for Chapter 6. Some of the dos and don'ts for implementing design choices are consolidated for the reader's consideration. The key point of this chapter is that it is not sufficient to have a good blueprint for organizational performance. One must also be skilled at managing the cultural and political norms when developing High Performance Organizations.

In Chapter 7, I offer a parting challenge to all who undertake the effort of redesigning their corporate future. The challenge is that the work of designing or redesigning organizations for high performance is never really finished. It is a never-ending cycle, more of a process in motion than a point of arrival. The theory, experience, and technology presented in this volume merely equip one to begin the journey.

Acknowledgments

This book has been importantly shaped and influenced by several people. I am most grateful to each of the following for their contributions, support, and friendship.

Dennis King, Laurence Megson, and Herb Stokes have been instrumental in helping me gain a practical understanding of Open Systems Theory and organization design. Herb and Dennis have also read manuscript drafts and provided helpful comments to improve its content. Laurence's unpublished working paper on Open Systems Theory served as the inspiration and role model for the introduction to systems theory in Chapter 1.

Arthur Jones first evolved the Organization Performance Model to its present form, and, with Barbara Sliter, helped with initial ideas on the Outside-In approach to organization design. Arthur's comments on the manuscript have also led to some important clarifications and improvements.

Ord Elliott did the early work on the subject of organizational diagnosis and design, which was a forerunner of the Organization Performance Model. His analysis of common issues facing most High Performance Organizations spurred me to begin thinking from the outside in. He has also provided some of the case studies that appear here and has made helpful comments on the manuscript. Ord and Abraham Shani provided the initial encouragement that eventually led to the writing of this book.

Craig Decker has been a trusted sounding board for many of the ideas outlined here. His comments on the manuscript have led to several improvements.

The Organization Performance Model has been influenced by several people over many years. Mike Crowther was the first to combine the processes of assessment and design into one model. Holger Krug and Ken Richardson helped refine the model.

Starr Eckholdt, Marc Forgas, Jose Miguel Gonzalez, and Ritchey Marbury provided some of the case studies in this book.

I must also acknowledge the influence of some key Procter & Gamble (P&G) managers with whom I have worked and who each epitomize high performance leadership: the late John Feldmann, Keith Harrison, Rolf Lengemann, Frank Myerscough, John Pepper, the late Wayne Richards, and Uwe Spiecker.

I am grateful to the Procter & Gamble Company for its cooperation in my undertaking. Those descriptions of examples that originated in the Procter & Gamble arena represent my own opinion, however, and do not necessarily represent the views of company management.

My thanks also to Dick Beckhard, Ed Schein, and Richard Hackman for their review of the manuscript and helpful suggestions to improve it. I am also deeply indebted to Dick for providing much-needed encouragement and support to help it happen.

The editorial staff at Addison-Wesley has been most cooperative and patient with me in bringing the final edition to press. Susan Badger, Jim Heitker, and Amy Kimball have been invaluable resources in the process. Helyn Pultz and Nancy Benjamin handled the editorial and production work.

Above all, I acknowledge my family—Charlee, Ben, Melanie, Angie, Beth, and Scott—without whose support this book would have never come about. I am grateful to them for their patience and understanding while Dad closeted himself away from their world to work on the Book.

Wyoming, Ohio   D.P.H.

Contents

1

Understanding How Organizations Function

An old French proverb states, *"The fish only knows it lives in water after it is already on the river bank."* And so it is with many who manage modern organizations. They are immersed in organizations every day. It seems that wherever they turn, they are transacting business with (or competing against) cartels, associations, corporations, agencies, or networks. All of these are organizations: groups of people working together to achieve some common purpose. Just as water is to the fish, organizations are our lifeblood, offering us the means to accomplish more than we could ever do alone. Yet many managers also struggle against the flow of activities, often frustrated by complex, bureaucratic ways. They exist in organizations, but seldom fully understand them. In some cases, like the fish on the river bank, they gain their understanding only after it is too late!

The more individuals work in organizations, the more certain phenomena continue to puzzle them, such as:

- Why does it take so long for important information to get from the top to the bottom of the organization and vice versa?

- Why is it that goals and priorities may be agreed upon in theory, yet in daily working life other goals and priorities are actually controlling the organization?
- Why do some organizations remain blind to threats to their survival, whereas these same threats are readily apparent to outsiders?
- Why do solutions to common problems work beautifully in some organizations but fail miserably in others?
- Why is it often difficult to get related organizations to cooperate on business priorities?
- Why is it that employees in large organizations often feel estranged and powerless, rather than as owners of the business?

One manager, reflecting on these and similar issues, said, "Everything would be perfect if it weren't for the organization!" He was voicing a frustration that may sound familiar to many. But as frustrating as organizations can be, avoiding them is not the way to relieve the pain. The only alternative is to better understand them and use that understanding to harness their full potential.

Many managers, I know, would give anything to be able to change their current organizational system and set up a new one that would deliver better results. That's what I believe high performance is — demonstrated results that are consistently superior over time. How does one set up such a system? Answering this question requires the exploration of two issues:

1. An understanding of the system as it is today.
2. The knowledge and skill to set up a system that will work better.

This chapter focuses on understanding systems (organizations) and introduces the technology for setting them up — the technology of organization design. First, it describes the nature of organizations based on Open Systems Theory and then discusses some ways this theory may help managers who wish to improve their organizations' effectiveness.

Why devote a chapter to theory in a book aimed specifically at practical application? As the following section highlights, our actions are usually based on some theory. The specific approaches described later in this book have their roots in Open Systems Theory. Too often we hear about successful techniques and try to reapply them in our own setting without fully understanding the theory or principles involved. When unexpected problems arise, those who are grounded only in techniques may be ill-equipped to get back on track. It is often the understanding of the principle behind the technique that permits responses to keep the system on target. Consequently, I have chosen to lay the theoretical groundwork now before proceeding to specific applications.

Why Organization Theory Is Helpful

Kurt Lewin, a noted pioneer in the behavioral sciences, once observed. "There is nothing as practical as a good theory." He was referring to the fact that we must often rely on sound theory to help us formulate and execute successful action plans. For instance, could anyone imagine developing a new detergent or pharmaceutical remedy without a knowledge of chemistry? Or would we have confidence in a market share report if the research organization involved had no familiarity with statistical sampling theory?

Certainly specialists need to understand the theory of their chosen discipline. But there are also benefits gained when everyone understands the basic theory in areas related to their specific assignment. For example, it is helpful for managers in sales, advertising, research and development, and manufacturing to know the basics of one another's functions when they work together. Regardless of one's particular corporate assignment, all who work in organizations need to have a basic understanding of what they are and how they operate. It is this understanding that can help them move faster and keep pace with the opportunities and challenges of today by identifying where to make maximum improvement with minimum expenditure of energy.

Evolution of Organization Theory

Organization theory has been evolving gradually for centuries. For years the topic was of little concern to most, because the only organizations of any substantive size and power were the state, the military, and the church. The Industrial Revolution changed all that as it brought together for mass production machines and multitudes of people to run them. Suddenly large industrial organizations began to spring up everywhere. This forced managers to examine the few referent organization models in an attempt to find some clues for organizing their mushrooming operations.

The organizational practices that emerged in this Machine Age have been labeled by some as *Machine Theory*. Indeed, many of this theory's premises stem from the assumption that an organization is like a machine: a collection of parts that need to be standardized and centrally controlled. The leading spokesmen for this theory were an American, Frederick W. Taylor (the father of Scientific Management),[1] and a German, Max Weber (creator of the Bureaucratic Model).[2] The common principles from their writings, which were the most widely accepted organizational practices until the post–World War II era, may be summarized as follows:

1. Tasks should be specialized and reduced to the smallest possible work cycle.
2. Work should be performed the same way every time.
3. Decision making should be exclusive to those in authority.
4. Uniform policies are needed to provide consistency.
5. There should be no duplication of functions — tasks should be handled exclusively by those assigned to them.

The monuments to this thinking are, of course, the assembly lines and the bureaucratic organizations formed to run them. There is little argument that production of goods increased dramatically as these systems sprang into operation. How much of this success was due to pure technological advances rather than organizational practices is debatable. At the time, however, the early successes seemed to uphold the principles of Machine Theory.

But as time wore on, Machine Theory ran into obstacles. Let's review briefly some of the unintended consequences that the five major principles caused.

1. *Task Specialization.* Work that was reduced to its smallest, most efficient cycle often became monotonous, degrading, and abusive to those who performed the tasks. "Monday cars" from the Detroit assembly lines and even more overt forms of production sabotage (graffiti; foreign materials packed into the product; missing parts) are familiar reminders of how workers have rebelled through the years against mundane work.

2. *Standardization of Performance.* Time and motion studies and other techniques were employed to find the one best way to do something. The only problem was, the "best" way for one did not always prove to be best for others. Even today in many organizations one of the most dreaded communiques is the work standard that requires employees in all departments to repair a gearbox or run a training session or conduct a performance appraisal following a standardized approach.

3. *Centralized Decisions.* This certainly provided unity of command, but often did not place decisions in the hands of those who were most knowledgeable. One of the common complaints about a bureaucracy is the delay that is involved while the person who could take action on an issue must wait for the hierarchy to pass judgment on it. One simple illustration of this is a typical procedure used by many department stores to authorize acceptance of a personal check as payment for merchandise. Invariably the cashier and customer must wait for an administrative person to come and approve the check so the transaction can be completed. In most cases, this person merely initials the check after recording some personal data about the check casher. Does this person do anything other than what the cashier

could have done to approve the check? Are the extra
time and expense justified by a better assurance that the
check will not bounce?

In most cases, such a step merely serves to preserve the decision-making rights of hierarchy. It also
contributes to inefficiency in the system. This example
is only a small problem when compared with many
others that cause companies to miss the "window of opportunity" in the market place. Frequently the unity of
command exacts a high price from the system by sepa-
rating decision making from the point where action
needs to be taken.

4. *Uniform Policies.* "That's what the book says" became
a standard slogan. All parts of the system were treated
in the same manner. Those individuals or operations
that had special requirements, needs, or performance
potential were merely asked to "get in line." Thus the
organization *earned* the image of being insensitive and
uncaring to specific employee and customers needs. It
was common in such situations for employees to turn
others away without solving their problem because procedures had to be followed.

But even worse, adhering to policy frequently became more important than the end result. No one was
expected to do less (or more) than the predetermined
minimum standard. Therefore the minimum also became the maximum that was achieved. Consider the
many documented episodes of employees restricting
production because there was no personal incentive to
do more or they feared the higher output would become
the expected norm. In such instances, "going by the
book" became the unassailable defense for holding back
effort.

A lab technician once explained to me how this
dynamic works. "If you abuse a person," he said to me,
"they will find a way to get even. Once a person stops
caring, they can put off your request or go only through
certain channels or by the procedure manual. They can
slow you down a lot."

5. *No Duplication of Functions.* Specialists emerged who became more devoted to their skill areas than to the success of the enterprise. "That's not my job" soon became the common reply (from skilled and unskilled alike) to any request for action that did not fit the segmented job structure. Thus everyone concentrated on their piece of the action, while much was lost in terms of overall quality, efficiency, and profitability.

The difficulties experienced with Machine Theory illustrate two main points:

1. A faulty theory (people are not machines) can lead to faulty execution and poor results.
2. A theory narrowly based on one set of circumstances may not fit other situations. Waging war, conducting religious worship, and mass-producing goods are vastly different tasks. For one organizational model to fit all, it must deduce the true common denominators from all situations. In retrospect, it is clear that Machine Theory tried to project the experience of a few into a model for all to follow.

Various other approaches to organization were taken in an attempt to "correct" the faults of Machine Theory. For example, the Human Relations movement began in the late 1940s as a counterbalance to the age of Machine Theory. This movement called attention to the forgotten needs of the people in the system. Interpersonal relations and management style were scrutinized in an attempt to humanize the workplace. Since that time we have been deluged by interventions and techniques that attempt to cure our organizational ills. Participative management, Management By Objectives, group dynamics, team building, quality circles, and visionary leadership are but a few of the tools (some might even call some of them fads) that have been introduced in the past four decades.[3] But no single approach has proved comprehensive enough to answer all of the questions or phenomena that the manager faces regularly.

Almost lost among all these theories was the argument in 1950 by an Austrian biologist, Ludwig von Bertalanffy, that previous approaches had focused too much on individual pieces of an organization (technical tasks, people, etc.) and not enough on the relationship of all of the pieces as they interact together. The theory espoused by von Bertalanffy (and rooted in biology) is known today as *General Systems Theory*.[4] It led to the classification of different types of systems, from mechanical and static systems to living systems. *Open Systems Theory*[5] is the framework that emerged from General Systems Theory to describe all living systems, including organizations. It is the most comprehensive existing model for describing all organizational elements and the dynamics of their interaction. Although it has been in the public domain for nearly four decades, this theory remains a hidden gem of an explanation for many managers in today's world of organizations.

The Organization as an Open System

The basic premise of Open Systems Theory is that organizations have common characteristics with all other living systems; from microscopic organisms, to plants, to animals, to humans. Understanding these characteristics allows us to work *with* the natural tendencies of an organization rather than struggle against them needlessly.

First let us define some terms. A *system* is an arrangement of interrelated parts. The words *arrangement* and *interrelated* describe interdependent elements forming an entity that is the system. Thus, when taking a systems approach, one begins by identifying the individual parts and then seeks to understand the nature of their collective interaction. It is the whole, not the parts alone, that counts.

All living systems are also classified as *open systems*. This means they are dependent on their external environment in order to survive and are, therefore, *open* to influences and transactions with the outside world as long as they exist.

The use of the word *open* in this context is frequently confused with open as in openness of communication and trust. It is important to keep these two meanings separate. *All organiza-*

tions are open systems as defined here. On the other hand, not every organization may have a climate of openness and trust. If an open system is an arrangement of interrelated parts interacting with its environment, what are the various parts if we focus on an organization? These may be summarized as follows:

1. *Boundary.* All systems have a border or *boundary* that differentiates them from others. This boundary may be physical (e.g., a building), temporal (a work shift), social (a departmental grouping), or psychological (a stereotyped prejudice). (See Figure 1–1.)

   Although the boundary tends to "fence off" one system from another, it has openings to allow for interactions with the environment. The degree of permeability (or openness) in the boundary is critical for the system's survival. Too much permeability can overpower the system with external demands, too little can cut off the system from needed resources.

2. *Purpose/Goals.* All living systems have a purpose, or a reason for existing. They are free to pursue their chosen course so long as they also fulfill certain expectations of their environment. (See Figure 1–2.)

   We see this in society every day. A great deal of latitude in personal values and life-styles is tolerated

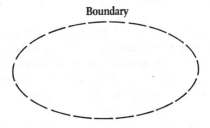

Boundary

Figure 1–1
Semi-permeable Organizational Boundary

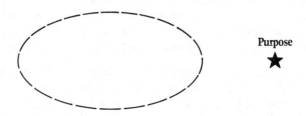

Purpose

★

Figure 1-2
Organizational Purpose

unless it leads to infringements on others, breaking laws, and so forth. We use the term *purpose* to refer to the organization's aim that meets its own, as well as environmental, needs. As such, the purpose is an implicit agreement or contract between the system and its environment that ensures the system's survival if fulfilled.

A corporate purpose statement, for example, would be incomplete if it focused solely on profits. Although this may be the main reason for existing (in the corporation's eyes), this is not the way the environment views it. The environment expects either goods or services that it values and it expects them to be delivered under certain conditions (ethical dealings, no pollution, etc.).

Certainly every product marketing group is familiar with the balancing act required to get its marketing strategy (or purpose) right. Maximizing profit while ignoring consumer demands for improved benefits poses a serious risk for the product's survival. On the other hand, meeting consumer needs without meeting the corporation's basic expectations (profit margin, growth, etc.) may cause the product to be discontinued.

The purpose is the contract with the environment; goals are specific internal targets established by

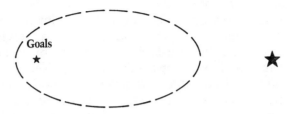

Figure 1-3
Organizational Goals

the system to guide its progress toward fulfilling the
purpose. (See Figure 1–3.) Together, the purpose and
goals provide two reference points for the organization
to define the critical or core tasks of its operation.
3. *Inputs.* Materials and energy must be imported from the
environment. (See Figure 1–4.) Just as the body takes
oxygen and food from its environment in order to survive and grow, so an organization draws on the outside
world for raw materials, money, equipment, market
data, ideas, and people. Failure to import sufficient mat-

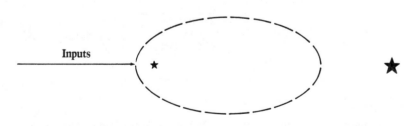

Figure 1-4
Inputs to an Organization

ter and energy resources leads to termination and death of the system.

4. *Transformation or Throughput.* The inputs must be transformed into other forms (products, services) in preparation for transformation and return to the environment. Product specifications are developed, goods are manufactured, advertising copy is produced, orders are assigned — in other words, *work is performed.* (See Figure 1–5.) The transformation is accomplished by the joint interaction of three core processes (*core* means something directly related to the purpose). These core processes are task, individual, and group. The *task core process* refers to the tasks required to achieve the purpose. The term *individual core process* describes the process whereby an individual focuses his or her energy on the fulfillment of the core tasks. How well individuals and core tasks are linked together is a function of the *group core process.* This process refers to how individuals divide tasks, communicate, and interact with one another. Work (or more precisely, *core work*) is accomplished by the combination of these three core processes.

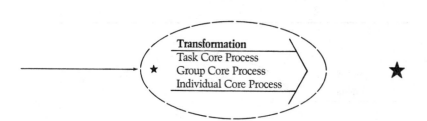

Figure 1–5
The Organization's Transformation Process Is Comprised of Three Core Processes

In a purchasing department, for example, price estimates from suppliers have to be gathered, negotiations handled, contracts finalized, orders placed, activities with the distribution department coordinated, and so on. These are elements of purchasing's task core process (as compared with tasks such as training, budgeting, or filing, which are all important but not in the core stream).

These tasks are performed by people who all have individual needs. Some may be thoroughly energized and excited by their work, others may be bored or frustrated. The individual core process reflects an overlap between what is important to the individual (needs and interests) and to the system (core tasks). When an individual works hard on the right things with obvious enthusiasm, that person is motivated. In reality, the person's personal energy and interest are focused on the core tasks of the system. Thus, a person who enjoys the challenge of negotiation is a motivated buyer. Someone else may be frustrated in price negotiations, but motivated by other core tasks.

The group core process, therefore, becomes important in dividing tasks and providing effective work relationships so that individual energy is tapped and the work gets done. Department meetings, office layouts, reporting relationships, work climate norms — all are elements of the group core process.

The challenge for any manager is to balance these three core processes to optimize results. This message may not seem new, but my experience suggests there are not many who are really successful at doing it. It is not enough to be aware of the core processes. What is required is a truly pragmatic way of balancing the core processes. As we will see in later chapters, specific changes in the way work is structured can accomplish this.

5. *Outputs.* Materials and energy (products, skills, services, etc.) are exported to the environment, hopefully

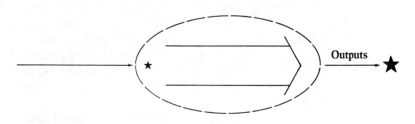

Figure 1–6
Organizational Outputs Targeted to Fulfill the Purpose

fulfilling the purpose contract. (See Figure 1–6.) Outputs also include undesirable by-products (pollution, scrap, rework, errors, etc.) in addition to those desired.
6. *Feedback.* Knowing whether or not the system is on target is a function of feedback. This term refers to information inputs that measure the acceptability of both outputs and the purpose and goals. The terms *negative* and *positive* feedback, from the field of cybernetics, distinguish between two important types of feedback. Negative feedback measures whether or not the output is on course with the purpose and goals. It is also known as *deviation-correcting* feedback. (See Figure 1–

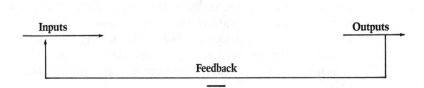

Figure 1–7
Negative Feedback Loop Comparing the Quality of Output to Goals

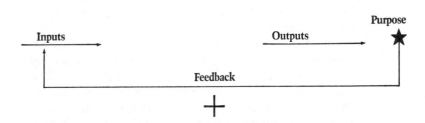

Figure 1-8
Positive Feedback Loop Comparing the Purpose to Environmental Needs

7.) Positive feedback measures whether or not the purpose and goals are aligned with environmental needs. It is sometimes called deviation-amplifying feedback. (See Figure 1-8.)

As an example, let's suppose a rocket has been fired and is targeted to land in the Atlantic Ocean. The rocket's path could be carefully tracked in relation to the targeted destination. This tracking system is an example of negative feedback. As long as the rocket remained on track, no action would be called for. If the rocket were to deviate from its intended course, the feedback system would alert us immediately. Now let's assume the target were to be changed from the North Atlantic to the South Atlantic. The rocket would receive a new signal, indicating it should deviate from its present course and aim for a different target. This is an example of positive feedback. It's hard to separate the meanings of *negative* and *positive* feedback in systems theory from their everyday connotations of bad and good. If our promotion campaign has yielded targeted shipments to the trade, this is (in systems theory) negative feedback *because it monitors whether the target is met or not.* But a blind test result that shows our product to be at a disadvantage to competition (even though everything was executed as designed) is positive feedback. *It tells us our contract with the consumer must be renewed.*

Does it really make any difference whether we label feedback as positive or negative, or is it merely an intellectual exercise for scientists and theorists? The usefulness of the two concepts is that they demonstrate that it is not enough to merely measure our outputs versus the intended targets. Survival of the system is equally influenced by whether or not the targets themselves are appropriate. By monitoring both signals, we can avoid the pitfall of reaching our targets, only to find the output is no longer valued sufficiently to keep the system alive.

7. *Environment.* By definition, everything outside the system's boundary is the environment. (See Figure 1–9.) The system must interface with various segments of the environment in order to survive. (An interface is an exchange of inputs or outputs.) This is the key difference between closed systems and open systems. Those who view an organization as a closed system make the major mistake of ignoring the environment. In reality, the environment provides the inputs, must accept the

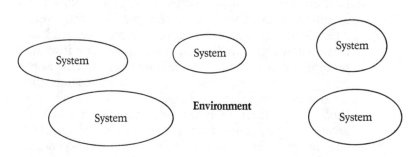

Figure 1–9
An Organization's Environment Is Made Up of Other Systems

outputs, must support the purpose, and provides feedback to the system. Thus, its influence on the life of the system is critical.

Although everything outside the system is its environment, not everything is equally relevant to the system's purpose and survival. Where the system's boundary is drawn determines what is relevant. For example, a television network will be very much concerned with the policies and regulations of the Federal Communications Commission; a pharmaceutical company will be similarly concerned with the Food and Drug Administration; both will be concerned with the Internal Revenue Service. Thus, the relevant components of government in a system's environment will vary according to its purpose. An organization may choose how it wishes to manage the key influences in its environment:

1. It may try to ignore the environment (e.g., closed systems thinking).
2. It may seek to control the environment (very difficult to do with *all* interfaces).
3. It may seek to balance the needs between itself and the environment.

Finding the "right balance" means the system may:

1. Cause changes in the influences/functions of some external groups.
2. Change its own operation in response to critical outside requirements.
3. Change its relationship with others by redefining workloads, expectations, purposes, communication patterns, etc.

The key point here is that managing the environment involves work — tasks that have to be planned, organized, and carried out just as internal tasks do. Managing the environment is also an iterative task due to the changing nature of today's environment. Thus, an organization needs to give constant attention to its relationships with environmental groups.

Dynamic Processes of a System

The seven items described above are critical elements of an organization as viewed from a systems perspective. The diagram in Figure 1-10 offers a static model (a snapshot) of these elements in relation to each other. I said earlier, however, that an important part of a systems approach is to understand the *dynamic interaction* of the various elements.

In other words, this living open system (the organization) exists through time. As it exists, the parts of the system interact with one another. Thus, the systems approach helps us in viewing organization as a process — a moving, changing network of connections existing through time; a chain of events. Unfortunately this movement is impossible to diagram in a two-dimensional book. What I can do is describe some of the dynamic processes and leave you to imagine the motion picture effect this would have on the static model. Five fundamental systems processes are:

1. *Information coding.* The discussion of feedback indicated that a system needs information to know whether its outputs and purpose are acceptable or not. There is always information available to a system on these issues. The key here is for the system to select the critical elements about which to seek feedback and to devise ways of monitoring these information channels. The reception of input is selective — systems can react only to those signals to which they are attuned. This is information coding — the programming of the system to respond to certain signals and to ignore others. (See Figure 1-11.)

   Much like a computer, the organization is programmed to sift through data and present only what is desired. Coding also determines the permeability of the boundary. The coding process is evident as you go through your mail: some items are discarded immediately, whereas others are studied in great depth.

   Information coding also explains, in part, why organizations seem to ignore signals from the environ-

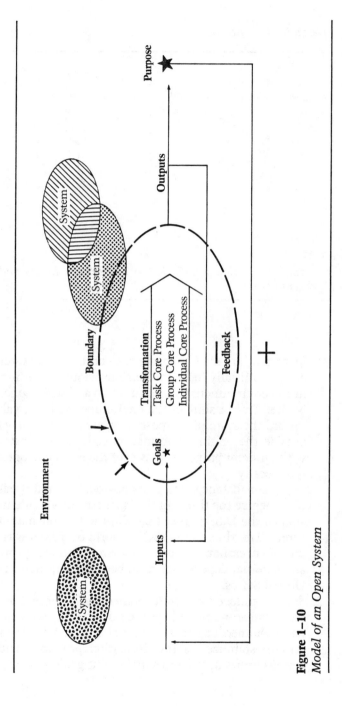

Figure 1–10
Model of an Open System

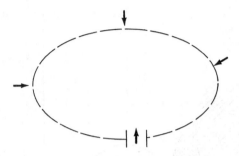

Figure 1–11
An Organization's Boundary Is Coded to Block Some Inputs and to Allow Others to Enter

ment that are readily apparent to others. The system's purpose initially leads to decisions about which inputs in the environment to be attuned to and which ones to ignore. Thus a shift in the environment's basic values toward the system's purpose may be missed; it may fall outside the original information code. Other systems, with different purposes, may spot the new development more easily.

For instance, observers obviously found it easier to recognize the threat of the Japanese automobile invasion to the U.S. market than did the Detroit manufacturers. The threat of OPEC to world oil prices was appreciated earlier in Europe (where historically prices and external dependence have been higher) than in the United States.

2. *Steady state or dynamic homeostasis.* From homeostatic, meaning thing kept the same, steady state or dynamic homeostasis is the natural tendency for the system to stabilize its transformation processes within certain limits in order to survive. The goals and purpose

provide "peg points" for a system to define a path for effective operation. Although performance ideally would not deviate at all from the targets, the system usually can bear some minimal deviations without serious consequences to purpose and goal accomplishment. This is diagrammed in Figure 1–12. An initial disturbance in an organism results in mobilization of energy to restore the balance, and recurrent upsets lead to actions to anticipate the disturbance. This basic principle in an organization is the tendency toward *self-preservation of the character of the system.*

A manufacturing operation illustrates this steady-state process clearly. If the target efficiency is 80 percent (and the system can tolerate approximately 5 percent variation), equipment is designed, staffing levels established, people trained to meet the target. If efficiency is 78 percent, the system attempts to make minor improvements. Individuals may receive specialized training on the few most nagging problems; engineers may help modify a piece of equipment to increase effi-

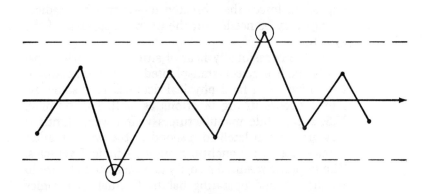

Figure 1–12
Homeostatic Forces Attempt to Keep the Operation within Acceptable Limits

ciency. But the system is able to meet the needs of its environment without much strain.

Should the efficiency fall below 75 percent, however, something else has to be done or else shipments may lag behind sales commitments. More specialists may be deployed on different work shifts, stricter material specifications may need to be enforced with suppliers, more intensive training may be needed, or extra staffing may be required until performance returns (and stays) at the required levels.

If the output jumps to 90 percent efficiency, we may have another problem. Now the cases produced may continually exceed what can be sold and expensive inventories will begin to stack up. Eventually equipment may need to be shut down or employees redeployed until the total output levels out within tolerable limits.

This characteristic of social systems also shows why it is so hard to change the way in which a particular organization unit functions: the unit will work toward maintaining its own character, which could well defeat the intended change. In other words, the system exerts so much energy to maintain stability, that it will oppose all forces that threaten it — even when radical change may be needed for the ultimate survival of the system.

We occasionally hear of situations in which patients' bodies reject transplanted organs that would have reversed a fatal physical decline. This same dynamic occurs in organizations as well. For example, U.S. automobile manufacturers waited years (until it was almost too late!) to respond to the world market demand for better quality, more fuel-efficient vehicles. The response required a costly and traumatic change in technology and operating habits. German electronics and photographic producers, once the industry trendsetters, continually ignored the presence of lower priced, high quality Japanese competitors in Europe. The German firms called for import restrictions rather than develop newer, more competitive products. Swiss watchmakers reluctantly replaced their fine timepiece mechanisms with quartz movements only after their market shares dropped to an all-time low. The simple truth is that the market place was sending a signal to these organizations that, if heeded, would have disrupted their state of equilibrium. This signal was ignored until the consequence of avoiding it meant certain loss of sales and even the demise of whole businesses.

3. *Negative entropy.* To survive, open systems must move to arrest the entropic process. Entropy is a principle describing all systems' movement toward disorganization and death. Biological organisms break down and die. Complex physical systems move toward simple random distribution of their elements. The organization is no different unless it imports more energy from its environment than it uses both in keeping itself going and in exporting back to the environment. It can therefore store energy and arrest the entropic process: it achieves negative entropy. This is a key difference between an organization and other living systems. Plants, animals, and humans can only prolong the entropic process for a certain amount of time before they die (see Figure 1–13). However, the organization may renew itself as

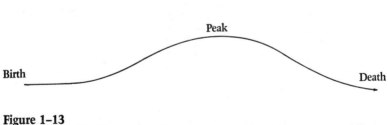

Figure 1–13
The Normal Life Cycle

long as its outputs generate sufficient new inputs from the environment. Thus, the life cycle of the organization may look more like Figure 1–14.

Although all organizations have this potential, not all of them fulfill it. Many organizations follow a normal biological life cycle. Some even fail to outlive their founders. In such cases, their output becomes no longer valued by the environment, demand for their goods or services dwindles, and the system perishes. There are numerous examples of this: buggy whips, slide rules, and candle lanterns to name some. Any company whose profitability was tied solely to these products soon became obsolete as new inventions took their place. The only way to prevent this decay from happening is to periodically monitor the system's outputs against what the environment needs (i.e., develop an effective positive feedback loop). Most product improvements are usually made in response to positive feedback from the environment.

4. *Equifinality.* The term *equifinality* refers to the fact that systems can reach the same final state from a variety of initial conditions and by a variety of paths. This adaptive capacity, or flexibility to get the job done, is evident in all living systems. Trees grow in different

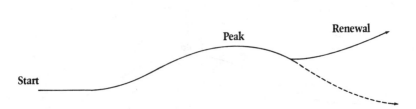

Figure 1–14
Organizations Are the Only Living Systems Who Can Renew Themselves Indefinitely and Thwart Entropy

patterns, following various sunlight patterns for nourishment. Office workers cope in the short term when a flu epidemic knocks out a third of the work group. These examples remind us of the old adage that "there is more than one way to skin a cat." There are many ways to achieve a result, depending on one's circumstances. The key point here is that open systems are *self-regulating* in terms of organizing their core processes to achieve their purpose. Artificial attempts to regulate the system's performance from outside run the risk of thwarting the system's natural instinct for self-preservation. Does this mean that self-regulating systems *always* respond as needed to achieve their purpose? The answer is no. In some cases feedback systems are not adequate to alert the system to danger, or coding leads us to ignore the signals that are present. In other situations *individual purposes* may differ significantly from the organizational purpose. This explains why some individuals may not react as needed by the system. They will always do what is relevant for their purposes; this may or may not be what the system needs. External coercion and control may help improve things for the short term, but is always an unnatural, second-best option. The general principle still holds true: open systems are self-regulating in pursuing *their* purposes.

5. *Specialization.* As systems grow, they become more elaborate and form new specialized functions to cope with the growth and to maintain the steady state. Just as cells divide, multiply, and develop more specialized functions over time, so organizations create new departments and additional specialist roles as they grow. The inherent problem of highly specialized organizations is that they, like all systems, resist changes or disturbances that appear to threaten their steady state. Thus, specialized subsystems work to preserve themselves as systems in their own right — even if their purpose has changed and the environmrnt has different needs from the parent system. For example, specialist bureaucratic functions now exist in the British Navy that were un-

dreamed of in the early 1900s (even though there are fewer sailors and ships now!).

Using the Theory to Improve Results

With an understanding of the basic principles of Open Systems Theory, you are now in a position to think in terms of systems when analyzing organizational issues. We all face situations in which we would like our organizations to respond or perform better. Systems theory can help in planning such improvements. To understand any system's (or subsystem's) functioning, we might begin by asking a few fundamental diagnostic questions:

1. What is the apparent purpose or goal of the organization that causes activities to be coordinated into a pattern?
2. What are the key outputs and their major boundary transactions?
3. What are the key conversion or transformation processes and how effectively are they balanced in achieving the purpose?
4. What are the key inputs and their major boundary transactions?
5. What is the reactivating feedback being delivered, both positive and negative?

Reviewing these questions is like conducting a health checkup for the organization. If the parts of the system are found to be well defined and functioning properly, the initial diagnosis is encouraging. If something were missing or didn't fit properly, corrective action might be required. (*Fit* refers to the condition in which all organizational elements are congruent with the intended results.)

The next phase is to diagnose what happens when the system moves or exerts itself — do all of the parts still function properly? Examining the key processes would lead us to ask such questions as:

1. *Information coding.* Does the system obtain the needed information inputs (e.g., feedback) and appropriately block out unneeded items?

2. *Steady state.* Is the system able to maintain its operation within the limits of tolerance related to its targets?
3. *Negative entropy.* Is the system able to import more than it exports by changing purpose, goals, and practices to match emerging environmental demands?
4. *Equifinality.* Is there capacity for self-direction and spontaneous self-regulation by individuals and groups to achieve the needed results?
5. *Specialization.* Does the system grow and expand appropriately without becoming overspecialized?

Again, depending on any processes that were found to be off target, corrective action would be needed.

Once the entire analysis has been made, you will have a clearer idea of why the organization's performance and results may be falling short in a particular area or areas. The theory can also be useful in giving pointers on the types of interventions or solutions that may be required to achieve levels of high performance. Because Open Systems Theory describes actual characteristics of social organisms, any initiatives we attempt should be developed with these characteristics in mind.

Avoiding Common Fallacies

Above all, systems theory can help the manager avoid many of the common fallacies based on incorrect or incomplete notions of what an organization is. The most common fallacies individuals are guilty of when managing open systems are:

1. *Treating a living, organic system (an organization) as if it were a lifeless piece of machinery.* This chapter has already discussed Machine Theory as being the predominant organizational model for more than two centuries. Most managers are appalled by the rigidity and dogma of Machine Theory when they see its principles listed. Yet they manage by these principles every day! The real problem with Machine Theory is that its mechanistic procedures work against a living system's natural tendencies so as to limit its potential effective-

ness and output. Improving this situation calls for a redesign of organizational patterns based on characteristics of living systems.

2. *Assuming that the organization's goals are also the goals of the individuals in the organization.* This is usually not the case, unless the goal-setting process somehow clearly identifies individual and organizational needs and then establishes end points that will cause one set of needs to be satisfied in the pursuit of the other.

3. *Ignoring the complex environment and looking only inside the system for planning and problem solving.* This overlooks important influences that the environment has on inputs, outputs, purpose, and feedback. The amount of complexity, interdependence, and uncertainty in the environment also has a major influence on the organizational structure required by the system to be successful. Open Systems Planning and the Outside-In approach to designing organizations (see Chapter 4) are useful in giving proper consideration to the system's relationship to the environment.

4. *Looking for one best way to handle a situation.* Generally there is no one best way. When evaluating action proposals, managers should pay more attention to whether the proposed actions will lead to the desired results rather than insisting that different groups all follow the same plan.

5. *Believing in a singular cause and effect relationship between variables when in most cases there are many causal factors.* Systems thinking helps us identify multiple causes and effects and to understand the patterned relationships involved.

6. *Dealing with only a piece of the total system while ignoring the impact on the whole.* Too often the piece is not considered in context of the whole, nor is there consideration given to the total system. We have been taught to handle one thing at a time, instead of seeing and dealing with the big picture.

7. *Treating irregularities in the system as though they were errors in performance when in some cases they might be caused by changes in the environment.* Two distinct feedback loops are needed to clarify if performance is unacceptable because the target has been missed (negative feedback) or to a movement in the target (positive feedback).

8. *Forgetting that the reason for existence (purpose) of the organization is also determined by the environment, not by the organization alone.* Open Systems Planning and the Outside-In approach can help align the two sets of interests (system and environment) into an effective sense of purpose.

9. *Not realizing that people, as open systems, are also self-regulating and usually function in an optimal manner when the following items exist:*

- Goal clarity
- Goal commitment
- Reasonable autonomy
- Clear feedback

The challenge here is to design a work system so that these four elements are present for all members of the organization.

10. *Believing motivation is something to give others* (i.e., it is extrinsic), rather than something that is intrinsic to individual energy level and interests. The question is not so much how to motivate someone, but how to create the conditions so that the person's energy and interests are tapped by the work to be done.

11. *Assuming people are uncooperative, when in fact they may have different goals.* Cooperation and teamwork require clarity of joint goals and expectations and constant monitoring of outputs versus the agreed targets. Handling these tasks should be a primary concern of managers.

12. *Spending much time measuring the results versus the purpose, but too seldom questioning whether the purpose itself is still appropriate.* As already covered, an

effective positive feedback loop will alert the system to environmental changes, which may make the current purpose obsolete.

13. *Ignoring the group core process by issuing directives and then depending on individuals to get the job done — somehow.* Ensuring that roles, activities, and communication patterns all fit together to accomplish the task is one of the functions of organization design.

14. *Not recognizing that resistance to change is almost always connected with the system's natural tendency to preserve its state of equilibrium* (homeostasis, information coding, etc.). Overcoming this requires a redefinition of purpose and goals and clear feedback.

15. *Failing to distinguish between accountability and responsibility.* The Unity of Command principle from Machine Theory exemplifies the ineffectiveness that creeps in when these two concepts are blurred together. In fact, accountability and responsibility are quite different as they occur in daily activities. Accountability can never be delegated. A leader is accountable for everything that goes on within an organization. But that doesn't mean that responsibility for what is done can't (or shouldn't) be placed on those who actually do the work. Being held responsible for one's work simply means that the individual shares the fruits of success and is expected to correct any errors that are made. It is precisely this sense of responsibility that meshes individual purposes with the organization's purpose and establishes the condition where self-regulation can be harnessed.

16. *Getting caught up in the core work, rather than making management's unique contribution through "boundary management."* The predominant role for many managers through the years has been that of supervisor. A supervisor is immersed in core work, checking the work of employees, and issuing instructions to them on what needs to be done next. This role model is another relic from Machine Theory.

There certainly are situations (e.g., when the core processes are not meshing) that require supervision. However, if that is all the manager does, the world of organizations will pass him or her by. Boundary management is a term that has been coined to describe the role of the manager in working interfaces with the environment, maintaining feedback channels, coordinating work with other departments, clarifying purpose, responding to change, and improving structures. Dr. W. Edwards Deming, the genius behind Japan's industrial juggernaut, has referred succinctly to the difference between boundary management and supervision as "working *on* the system rather than working *in* the system."

An Example of High Performance

With an understanding of Open Systems Theory and an appreciation for the common fallacies that have restrained complex organizations to date, we now have a framework to begin improving a system. Before charging off, however, let's stop to ponder one question.

What would a High Performance Organization look like?

Let me cite an actual example of high performance that may be typical of those who will be the successful organizations in the next century.

The owner of a small civil engineering firm, MARCO, was facing a crisis in his business. After years of plentiful contracts and major project work, the construction business had dropped off drastically in the recession of the early 1980s. MARCO's reputation for quality work was unparalleled in the area, but there simply wasn't much work to be contracted out. MARCO and its competitors were all struggling to keep their staffs fully occupied. From its humble beginnings as a family operation, MARCO was expanded by fifteen staff members in the 1970s to handle an annual contract volume of $26 million. Now the work load required only half the number of draftsmen, surveyors, and engineers that were on the payroll.

The choice appeared to be a simple one. Cut the staff and regroup the remaining resources to handle the reduced workload. But the owner hesitated. This small business team was now like part of the family. They had all gone beyond the call of duty on numerous occasions in the past. And who could know when the business slump would end and these employees would be needed again? In desperation, the owner considered what other things MARCO could deliver that would make a profit and keep the employees on the payroll.

One day, while traveling on business to a distant city a place mat in a diner caught his attention. The place mat had a number of advertisements on it for other local businesses — dry cleaners, hairdressers, auto mechanics, and the like. The place mat was simple, yet tastefully done. The artwork and lettering were sketched by an artist and then reproduced in different colors. "Why, my draftsmen could do a better job than that," the owner said to himself. Small advertising contracts like this could be quite lucrative if enough of them were combined together, in one project, he thought. The skills required were primarily in marketing, sales, and graphic art. The owner knew he had the graphic art skills. He and many others were experienced in marketing and selling to customers because they had to negotiate for contracts against other very strong competitors. His firm's track record of making the sale had been impressive.

The owner began his own market research study. He discussed the prospects of such a venture with many restaurants and diners not only in his own city, but in several neighboring ones as well. He also probed the possible interest of small businesses to advertise in such a venture on an ongoing basis. After some weeks of investigation, the prospects seemed very promising. Only one obstacle remained — would the employees be willing to shift their jobs' focus? Would draftsmen sketch out advertisements rather than blueprints? Would surveyors be willing to call on clients to collect accounts? Would they all be willing to approach small businesses to sell accounts?

Much to his delight, the owner found his employees were willing to do all of these things. It was gratifying to learn how committed his staff was, not only to him but also to the firm. Each employee expressed a commitment to do whatever necessary to secure his or her job and help MARCO survive the tough times. None of them wanted to see it lose its prestige or the potential to lead the way when the market rebounded.

The transformation began. All those who were not needed on design contracts were assigned to the new advertising arm of the business. This new operation took off well and was able to compensate for the loss of design contracts. Due to the profitable new business, the firm was able to keep its head above water at a time when some of its competitors either went under or drastically curtailed their operations. Of thirteen firms who were competing before the recession, only MARCO avoided going out of business or merging with a larger company.

In time, construction began to boom again. The owner was then able to redeploy all of his people in the civil engineering business. He sold the advertising franchise to the salesman who had been hired to make the new venture successful in the first place. MARCO came out of the whole experience considerably stronger than before the recession. The recession had actually worked to MARCO's advantage. At a time when other firms were laying off top people, MARCO had hired some of those people to handle the advertising and civil engineering arms of the business. Net, MARCO had the most skilled work force in the industry in the local area. It alone was able to staff the new projects, while its competitors had to start from scratch for the new cycle.

So what does this small business have to do with the large organizational issues we have been discussing? Certainly the specific situation was different for MARCO than for many others. The point I am making with this example has nothing to do with organization size or industry structure. It illustrates responsiveness and survival skills. Every manager should ask the question, "Could my organization respond this way tomorrow if a recession hit our business?" Despite the uniqueness of its particular situation, MARCO is a good model of some remarkable survival skills:

- The *ability to read the business situation* and recognize that current staffing and products would not survive. This is an excellent example of utilizing appropriate information coding and positive feedback to save the enterprise.

- The *ability to sense new business opportunities* in the environment that called for skills it already possessed. The firm was able to redefine its purpose to fit the environmental reality.
- A remarkable degree of *flexibility* to rearrange its operation to manage the existing and new businesses. This small system balanced its task, individual, and group core processes effectively to support its new purposes.
- A sense of *ownership among employees.* They were all entrepreneurs who had a stake in the success or failure of the company. Everyone could see how their efforts made a difference to the enterprise. They were successful in self-regulating their efforts against the core tasks to ensure organizational survival.

The bottom line, of course, is that these survival skills made MARCO a high performer. It achieved negative entropy in a time when casualties were high in its industry. Its results were consistently superior to its competition — even in the most trying of times.

I believe these same characteristics will be needed by many organizations in the future. The question is: are there ways of developing these survival skills in larger organizations? So much of this seems natural when one has a small operation. The problem comes when the organization gets big and procedures become formalized along the lines of Machine Theory.

In my experience, there are ways of developing organizations of any size to be high performers. Consider some of the well-documented examples[6] such as:

- Gaines' Pet Food plant in Topeka, Kansas, where work teams have produced high performance for over fifteen years.
- Digital Equipment's manufacturing plant in Enfield, Connecticut, where there are no supervisors, but performance is at industry-high levels.
- Mountain Bell, where telephone operators supervise virtually all aspects of their daily operation.

- Procter & Gamble's "technician plants," which have produced high performance in a variety of technologies for paper products, detergents, soap, snack foods, beverages, pharmaceuticals, and beauty care items.
- AT&T's American Transtech subsidiary in Jacksonville, Florida, where work groups have contributed to record productivity and error-free processing in issuing stock certificates.
- Tektronix's Portland, Oregon, facility, where an organization redesign project led to sharply improved results with an existing technology and workforce.

Such organizations combine the best of all qualities: they feel like small family businesses, yet are able to mass-produce for global markets. They are structured for consistency, yet can respond flexibly to new demands. They are made up of employees who, although cooperative team players, also have an entrepreneurial spirit to step out from the crowd. How do they do it? They don't do it by chance, and not by policy or decree. They do it by design.

Organization Design: One Key to High Performance

Many organizations have found through the years that they can influence their culture to produce the behavior (and results) they want by the way they design, or structure, certain aspects of their operation. For example, in the area of pay systems, we have learned:

- Pay based on seniority usually causes employees to remain in the system longer, but doesn't guarantee they will be highly motivated.
- Pay based on one's job title usually causes specialists to emerge who can handle their field of expertise well, but may not be committed to a continuous improvement in results.
- Pay based on contribution usually causes employees to focus more on results than activities, but can produce some culture shock when first introduced.

Ideally, the organization would consider what its business situation requires, what kind of culture its leadership values, and how it wants its employees to respond and then would design its pay system to support these requirements and desired values.

The challenge here is not to feel overwhelmed by the fact that there are so many elements of an organization's operation that need to be designed. Many don't feel like investing the time and energy into formally clarifying what their values are and designing their organizations to be congruent with these values. The interesting thing is that all of these elements do get designed, whether formally or informally.

For instance, in the absence of any pay guidelines, one foreman may choose to pay employees according to their contribution, while other foremen pay according to seniority or job title. A labor union may intervene and successfully negotiate for a common system based on seniority — and the design choice is made. We seldom view a contract bargaining process as an organization design effort, but that's exactly what it is. Whether the choice emerging from such a process fits the business and employee needs is often a forgotten question. Nonetheless, this design choice will have considerable impact on the organization's culture: what employees value, how they behave, and how focused their efforts will be on obtaining the needed business results. The organization's results are actually the bottom line of all the conscious and unconscious design choices that are exercised.

My good friend, Arthur Jones, has captured the impact of these dynamics in a very insightful phrase: *All organizations are perfectly designed to get the results they get!* For better or worse, the system finds a way of balancing its operation to attain certain results. The corollaries to this statement are:

1. *To get better results, you need to improve the design of the organization, and*
2. *If you change the design, be careful not to disturb what's working now.*

The approaches outlined in this book have been able to fulfill both of these conditions. They represent methods of putting open systems theory to work to develop high performance. They will assist the manager who, as an agent of change, is serious in the intent to create more effective ways of operating amidst complex and often changing environmental requirements. They are no panacea, but they do represent learnings from the past thirty years that have led to high performance in a variety of settings.

Notes

1. F. W. Taylor, *The principles of scientific management* (New York: Harper, 1911).

2. M. Weber, *The theory of social and economic organization* (trans. A. M. Henderson and T. Parsons), T. Parsons, ed. (New York: Free Press, 1947).

3. "Business fads: What's in — and out," *Business Week* (20 January 1986): 52–61.

4. K. E. Boulding, "General systems theory: The skeleton of science," *General Systems*, Yearbook of the Society for the Advancement of General System Theory 1:11–17; L. von Bertalanffy, "General system theory," *General Systems*, Yearbook of the Society for the Advancement of General System Theory, 1(1956):1–10.

5. L. von Bertalanffy, "The theory of open systems in physics and biology," *Science* 111(1950):23–28; F. E. Emery, ed., *Systems thinking* (Baltimore: Penguin, 1969); D. Katz and R. L. Kahn, "Organizations and the system concept," in *The social psychology of organizations*, 2nd ed. (New York: Wiley, 1978), 18–34; J. G. Miller, *Living systems* (New York: McGraw-Hill, 1978).

6. E. E. Lawler, III, "The new plant revolution," *Organizational Dynamics* (Winter 1978):2–12; T. O. Taylor, D. J. Friedman, and D. Couture, "Operating without supervisors: An experiment," *Organizational Dynamics* (Winter 1987):26–38; J. J. Sherwood, "Creating work cultures with competitive advantage," unpublished paper, 1987.

2

An Organization
Performance Model

In this chapter we will begin to examine some practical ways the manager can implement the principles of Open Systems Theory to produce a High Performance Organization. Developing high performance out of practices attuned to lower standards requires some fundamental changes in the way the organization operates. This is a formidable, but by no means impossible, task. Influencing a large organization can be successful if, like eating the proverbial elephant, one approaches it one bite at a time.

There are two processes that I have found to be absolutely critical for breaking down a large systems intervention and making it manageable. These processes are organizational assessment and design. My experience is that these processes, when managed well, can create truly high performing organizations. This chapter provides an introductory overview of these two vital processes. Each is examined in greater depth in Chapters 3 and 4 respectively.

It is important to keep assessment and design in their proper perspective. In order to do this, I want to digress for a moment and return to the organization design hypothesis stated in Chapter 1:

> *"All organizations are perfectly designed to get the results they get."*

Think about this statement for a minute. What it means is that every organization has ways of balancing out the many demands for its time, attention, resources, and energy. Depending on the balance that is struck, the system performs and delivers certain results. Think of this balancing act as *design*. Design is not just structure. It is not always formal or conscious. This balancing of resources isn't always fixed — you may not do things the same way every time and your results may vary (even drastically!) from month to month. But, you can't really argue with this statement— the fact that certain results occur (and not others) verifies that *some* design has been perfectly executed.

As also stated in Chapter 1, from this hypothesis spring two corollaries:

1. *To get better results, you need to improve the design of the organization.* Again, the term *design* here refers to more than just formal structure. It is describing this total balancing act of time, attention, resources, and energy.

2. *If you change the design, be careful not to disturb what's working well now.* Every design has some features that are worth keeping. Any change you contemplate will probably have both good and bad implications for whatever your current design and objectives are. This requires a careful and accurate assessment of how the system is currently operating and why.

To sum it all up, assessment is the process that tells the manager what is out of balance and what is functioning effectively. Design is the process whereby the manager balances organizational resources (inputs, goals, employee energy, task requirements, group dynamics, feedback mechanisms) to achieve results.

The decision to utilize either process presupposes that a change is needed (or may be needed) in organizational performance. Therefore, managers should consider an overall change strategy and have it clearly understood by relevant members of the organization before embarking on assessment or design. Each process is an intervention in itself. Each will require time, energy, and attention from several individuals. Whether the strategy is to correct known deficiencies or merely to enhance continuous improvement, the chosen objective will determine what the appropriate timing and methodology of either process might be. In other words, neither assessment nor design is something one takes off the shelf and uses mechanistically. Each is a tool that should be used as part of an overall change strategy.

The Organization Performance Model

There are many approaches to assessment and design. Let us look at one model that has been used successfully in a number of settings — the Organization Performance (OP) Model (See Figure 2–1). This is a framework for keeping in perspective five key variables that have an impact on organizational performance. This model is especially useful when one is attempting to understand why the organization's results are what they are (and not

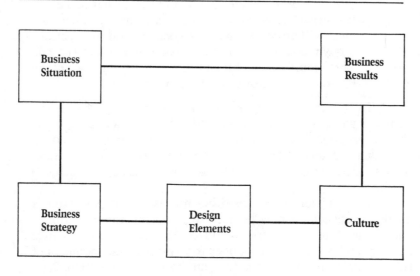

Figure 2–1
Brief Organization Performance Model

better) and to plan changes that will lead to improved results. Figure 2–1 illustrates organizational performance as an outcome that is influenced by how well the five critical factors are balanced (or fit) with one another. It also depicts the cause-and-effect chain that produces results — whether they be desirable or undesirable. What are the factors in this performance chain?

The first factor is the *Business Situation* facing the organization. This Business Situation is made up of elements and forces in the organization's *environment*. The environment has needs that the organization must satisfy; and also exerts pressures that must be managed. These needs and pressures may consist of such things as:

1. Expected hard number results.
2. Corporate expectations, such as budgets, growth patterns, rates of return, development of technology and people, and so on.
3. Social, political, or legal expectations from the environment.
4. Competitive pressures, such as new product innovations, pricing competition, and raw material shortages.
5. Expectations of employees and their families about such things as job security, career growth, levels of participation, and wages.

The Business Situation includes today's environmental needs and pressures as well as those that may have a strong impact on the organization in the future.

The second factor is the *Business Strategy*, or the organization's reason for being. Strategy in this context consists of the organization's purpose, goals, and underlying values and assumptions. All of these elements determine what's important in the system. They define what things will be done and what things won't be done. They also determine what the critical tasks of the system will be and on what members will focus their attention as they carry out their daily tasks.

The third factor is embodied as the *Design Elements*. This area is concerned with the organizational tools such as tasks and technology, structure, rewards, people, information systems, and decision-making processes, that are used to execute the business strategy. These tools provide structure to work tasks and reinforce patterns of behavior. How people are organized to do their work and how they interact with each other are both critical factors.

The *Culture* of the organization is the fourth factor. There are many definitions of culture in the literature today due to its particularly complex nature.[1] Culture is much like air; it is everywhere we look and touches everything that goes on in organizations. It is both a cause and an effect of organizational behavior. The more we learn about organizations, the more elements of culture we discover. There are behaviors, values, assumptions, rites, rituals, folklores, heroes, creeds, physical artifacts, and climate. All are elements of culture. Unfortunately, the definitions of culture that are the most inclusive are also the most esoteric and unwieldy to the manager. They cause many managers to shrug at the prospect of ever understanding — or managing — culture.

I propose a more limited, but pragmatic definition of culture to be used in the context of the OP Model. When focusing on the Culture box in the model, I prefer to think of culture as the observable *work habits and practices* that explain how the organization really operates. The way the system really operates is what produces results — whether they be good or bad. When viewed this way, culture is not some mystical phenomenon which has no relevance to effectiveness. On the contrary, it is a critical factor of organizational performance — and something every manager needs to understand. There is a "hidden" side of culture *(underlying values and assumptions)* which is included further upstream in the Business Strategy box because values and assumptions are causal forces that shape many of the other systems dynamics.

These two elements, (1) the behaviors and work patterns one can observe, and (2) the underlying values and assumptions that often cause the behaviors, are generally regarded by most theorists as core components of culture. Zeroing in on them simplifies things considerably. We can't fully understand everything about culture, but we can understand the essential behaviors and values. And these two elements have the most critical influence on results.

Finally, the actual *Business Results*, or outputs, being delivered currently by the system form the final factor. These results correspond to the same categories in the Business Situation. These are the key factors that affect performance. The model also depicts the cause-and-effect linkages that exist among the performance factors. Let's examine these linkages more closely.

Cause-and-Effect Linkages in the OP Model

First, let's consider the Business Situation–Business Strategy link. This link is evidence of how conscious the organization is of the environmental forces that will make or break it. An organization that ignores its environment will be characterized by several critical blind spots in its business strategy. New trends or expectations, which are critical for its survival, may be overlooked. In contrast, an organization that deeply recognizes its dependence on the environment for survival and growth will do whatever necessary to implement strategies and policies that accurately address key environmental expectations. It will also be able to adjust these strategies and policies appropriately as environmental conditions change. Thus, its strategy will always be a valid "contract" with the environment, which will ensure survival if fulfilled.

The Business Strategy–Design Elements link exposes some critical issues related to high performance. In discussing culture, I said it is both a cause and an effect of organizational behavior. Values and assumptions cause certain behaviors to play out in the system. They also shape priorities and behaviors as much as formal strategic documents; in many cases they have more influence than the formal strategies. In considering how to execute the chosen business strategy, managers will make decisions, based on their objectives and values, about such things as:

1. The tasks people do.
2. The structure within which they work.
3. How they are rewarded.
4. How decisions get made.
5. The information they use.

6. The people themselves, (meaning their basic abilities and motivations).

All of these elements are interrelated.[2] A change in one will undoubtedly produce some changes in the others. This is illustrated in Figure 2–2. These linkages, the very essence of organization, are too frequently ignored by managers.

The Design Elements–Culture relationship is another cause-and-effect link in the organizational performance chain. As I said earlier, the design choices tend to reinforce patterns of behavior. Thus, the design choices have a major impact on the organizational culture that will emerge. For instance, information practices which share vital business data only to the middle organizational layers will greatly influence the culture. Decision making delegated to the lowest possible levels will develop cultural patterns very different from systems in which all decisions are made at the top. Work that is structured according to Machine Theory will shape employee ownership and initiative differently than other structures. This design elements–culture chain reaction is the process that actually blends individuals, tasks, and group energy to yield results.

The Culture–Business Results connection links work behaviors in the organization with the results produced. "Nothing comes from nothing" goes the old German saying. Results are the outcome of what people in the organization do — tasks, habits, norms, standards, and practices. These are all elements of culture.

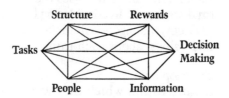

Figure 2–2
Interrelated Linkages among the Organization Design Elements

The Business Results–Business Situation is the last linkage. This measures the ultimate performance of the organization. It tells us how well the fundamental "contract" between the organization and the environment is being fulfilled. All other linkages merely contribute to this relationship.

The real utility of the OP Model lies not only in its depiction of the key variables influencing organizational performance, but also in illustrating the vital steps one must pursue when managing the processes of organization assessment and design. Let us now use the model to introduce the key steps of these two processes.

The Assessment Process

Conducting an assessment of organizational effectiveness is much like having a health checkup with the family physician. Just as we would expect a good physician to make a diagnosis of the patient's ailment before prescribing treatment, assessment should precede design or redesign. When assessing how effective the performance of the organization is, we begin with the Business Situation box in the OP Model and examine each connection in the performance chain by moving clockwise (see Figure 2–3).

The steps for conducting an organizational health checkup may be summarized as follows:

1. Compare current business results with the future business situation that the organization will likely face. This gives a fairly accurate reading of the organization's vital signs.
2. Examine the operating culture and norms to determine the symptoms of any malfunctioning, which will explain why the vital signs are what they are.
3. Analyze the organization design elements to gain a more penetrating look at the root causes of the culture.
4. Identify the actual operating strategy to understand the forces that have influenced the design elements.
5. Compare the actual operating strategy with the requirements of the business situation and note any areas of congruence or inconsistency.

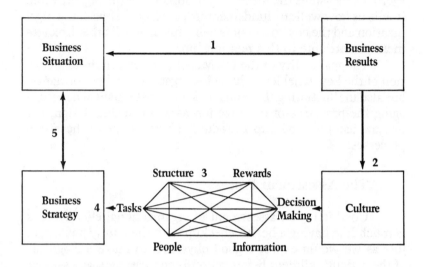

Figure 2–3
The Assessment Process

Having completed such an assessment process, much like undergoing a medical diagnosis, the manager is in a position to understand the state of the organization's health. Let's look at each of these steps in more detail.

1. Compare Current Business Results with the Future Business Situation

We begin by comparing the requirements imposed by the Business Situation with the Business Results actually delivered at present by the organization (see Figure 2–4). Given this comparison and any future requirements which may be known, we can determine which results need to change and which ones need to remain the same.

For example, a bottling plant was started up in the southwestern United States. The main thrust of its charter was to es-

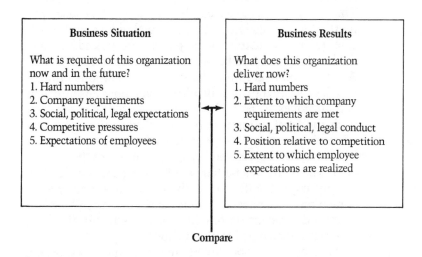

Figure 2–4
Comparing Business Results with the Business Situation

tablish a reliable capacity for the parent company's products. The major expectations for this plant (i.e., the business situation it faced) were to:

- Produce the product at a higher rate of efficiency than other plants (approximately 90 percent).
- Maintain the highest product quality standards achieved anywhere in the company.
- Cultivate a healthy employee relations climate and avoid any unnecessary third party interventions.
- Provide experienced leaders for anticipated future plant start-ups.
- Respond flexibly to changing production demands (schedule, product type) without serious drops in results.

At the time an organization assessment process was initiated, the plant's actual business results in these five areas were described as follows:

- Production efficiencies were at an average of 70 percent. This shortfall was unacceptable and felt to be caused primarily by a struggle to bring new technology on-line.
- The quality standards in the plant were indeed the best in the company (and better than the competition's).
- After a good beginning, the employee relations climate had deteriorated to an unhealthy level. Both absenteeism and turnover were higher than expected. Cooperation with the local union was limited only to those subjects where interaction was required by law.
- The experience level and leadership ability of the managers in the plant was far below what the company needed. Simply coping with the daily work targets fully consumed most managers' energies and time. The plant was heavily dependent on outside resources to set direction and manage changes to the business.
- The ability to respond flexibly to new situations was low. New developments overwhelmed the organization.

This comparison got the attention of the plant's leadership team. In reality, it did not reveal much new information. Most of these issues were already known, at least at some visceral level, by members of the system. The comparison did, however, focus attention on the key areas that needed improvement and traced the bottom-line implications of each. Once the implications of the status quo were more clearly understood, the plant's leaders were committed to pursue major improvements in the way the organization operated.

2. Examine the Operating Culture and Norms to Determine the Symptoms

Now we move down from results to Culture (see Figure 2–5). In this step, we examine only the attributes of how the organization really operates:

- The visible attitudes toward formal strategies and goals.
- Actual distribution of power and rewards.
- The actual work that people do or don't do.
- Other norms that explain how things get done or don't get done.

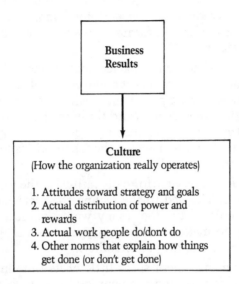

Figure 2–5
Tracing Cultural Causes of the Business Results

This is done by examining each result (good or bad) currently produced and asking the question, "Why?" Why is profit satisfactory? Why is quality below the acceptable level? Why is turnover rising in the last quarter? To answer each of these questions, we focus on observable daily behaviors.

For instance, a division of a major consumer products firm was puzzled by the fact that, despite healthy year-to-year volume growth, profits were not improving. Much time and attention were given to the subject in top management meetings and memos. An assessment process was begun and the following cultural attributes were identified as having the most influence on the daily operation:

Despite all the formal rhetoric about profitability, the key factor that captured everyone's attention and interest was market share. As soon as the latest share reports were issued, managers at all levels huddled around them like bees in a honeycomb. Conversely, profit improvement tracking was not uniform in format nor was it greeted with much enthusiasm.

There was no general agreement about how important profitability really was. Employees in all departments of the division were polled about what they thought the key priorities were. Aside from those in the headquarters, no department had more than one third of its employees who listed profit growth among the top priorities toward which they were personally working.

Most decisions were formally ratified at the top of the organization. This led to the feeling that decisions could be made only at the top. Many were skeptical about their ability to make something happen, even if they were to attempt to improve profitability.

Senior management spent little of its time in sessions to advance profit improvement projects. In contrast, they spent many hours of each day reviewing the latest marketing developments to improve market share.

The fundamental belief that drove everyone's personal energy was "Get the volume and the profits will follow." This strategy had served the division well in the past. There was strong resistance to changing it.

The unspoken rule in the system was "Promise whatever top management wants to hear; then deliver what you can." Forgiveness was easy to obtain when unforeseen factors impeded results. To consciously plan on results that were less than what management expected, on the other hand, was not acceptable.

Thus, the culture of this division was finely tuned to deliver volume, but not designed to deliver a discontinuity in profit.

3. Analyze the Design Elements to Understand the Root Causes of the Culture

Having identified the cultural elements that influence results, we now move into the Design Elements box (see Figure

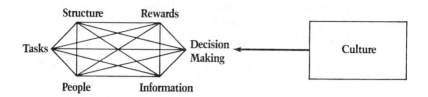

Figure 2-6
Tracing Organizational Design Elements as Causes of Cultural Attributes

2-6). This step in the process takes each element of culture previously identified and asks why these cultural elements exist. The answers are then sorted into each of the six design categories. Again, we can ask ourselves which of these design causes we want to keep and which we want to change.

One organization I am familiar with had an enviable record of meeting project commitments. Seeming miracles were regularly performed as complicated projects moved ahead and their deadlines were met. Time and time again, individuals would go to any lengths to get a project finished on time. "Why?" we asked. Here are the design elements that explain this phenomenon.

- *Structure.* Most employees were organized in project teams rather than in specialist pools. Consequently, they identified heavily with project success.
- *Rewards.* Those who didn't meet deadlines didn't move ahead careerwise.
- *Task.* All project activities were mapped out on a critical path format, with each activity clearly assigned to specific individuals.
- *People.* Every employee was carefully screened during the hiring process. They were high achievers who were extremely goal oriented.
- *Information.* The business rationale for each project was shared with team members. Each person understood how his or her contribution would have an impact on corporate results.

- *Decisions.* Teams were given much latitude in daily decisions as long as deadlines and standards were met. People felt responsible for what they produced and believed they could control their work.

As you can see, this organization is "perfectly designed" to complete projects on time.

4. Identify the Actual Operating Strategy to Understand the Forces That Have Influenced the Design Elements

Next, we ask ourselves why the particular design elements have been chosen. These design elements are chosen based on core values and assumptions. To find out what these values and assumptions are, we deduce what the Actual Operating Strategy is (see Figure 2–7). This is done by listing the tasks actually done in the organization and then deducing the strategies, values, and assumptions the system is actually following. This operating strategy does not always correspond to the published or agreed strategy, just as the organization's culture doesn't always match the formal organization chart.

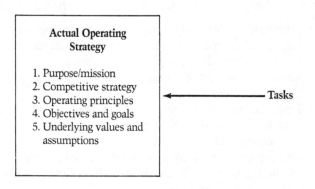

Figure 2–7
Tracing the Actual Operating Strategy as the Chief Cause of Design Element Choices

Let's return for a moment to the division that was troubled by its lack of profitability. The formal strategy was to radically improve profitability and maintain volume growth. But, as we saw in the cultural analysis, the actual operating strategy was more along the lines of "Get the volume and the profits will follow;" "Promise whatever top management wants to hear, then deliver what you can;" "Work harder — the same way we have always worked."

Now for the key point about strategy: the actual results of this division were much closer to the actual operating strategy than to the formal business strategy! Volume was progressing and profits were following (albeit very slowly). Forecasts were drawn up that met top management's expectations, but actual business performance seldom matched up to the forecasted level. Despite several experiments with new organization forms to accelerate profit improvement, the division usually reverted to its "bread and butter" way of operating.

As this example illustrates, gaining an accurate understanding of the actual operating strategy is absolutely critical for getting a fix on why today's results are what they are. As you can imagine, uncovering what really drives the organization is a tricky task. Many are not even aware of what actually drives them. Having generated the data in the previous assessment steps can be a great aid in making an accurate deduction of the actual operating strategy.

5. Compare the Actual Operating Strategy with the Business Situation

Figure 2–8 gives an assessment of the appropriateness of the operational strategy for the survival and growth of the organization. Where the operating values and priorities are a good fit with the business situation, no change may be called for. If this is not the case, adjustments will be needed or else the system will be working on the "wrong" things.

This can be a painful step. It is never pleasant to face the prospects of one's strategy, values, and assumptions being out of sync with the business situation. These issues usually represent deeply held convictions about the way the organization should function. But assessing the appropriateness of the operating strat-

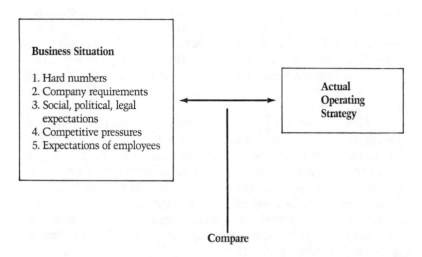

Figure 2–8
Comparing the Fit Between the Actual Operating Strategy and What the Business Situation Requires

egy can avoid being victimized by one's own blind spots. In the context of the assessment process described here, the assessor can build the logical cause-and-effect chains and show how they have an impact on the bottom line.

A clear example of the benefit of comparing the actual operating strategy with the business situation is the bottling plant in the Southwest. You will recall this plant was expected not only to master its current manufacturing process, but also have the capability of debugging new technologies and exporting leaders to future start-ups. Yet, one of the operational strategies in the plant was, "Leave us alone!" Scarcely a day went by without a member of the leadership team saying, "If they [the company] would just leave us alone, we could improve our daily efficiencies." The disruptions, of course, were key elements of the business situation (new product forms, equipment changes, transfers to other plants, etc.) that were not going to go away. Once this business situation was clearly understood, the leadership team saw the fallacy of its operating strategy. It was then prepared to make some revisions.

This completes the assessment process. Having gone through it, the organization should now have a better understanding of why its results either fit or don't fit the business situation it faces. And it should be clear about which organizational elements are helping or hindering high performance.

The Design Process

Just as a prescription can be made following a thorough medical diagnosis, a plan to improve the organization's health can be made after the assessment process has been completed. This prescription in organizational terms is to design, or redesign, the various organizational elements so that the organizational body begins to function more effectively. *Effectively* in this sense means that the results produced are up to the requirements of the business situation. The ideal, of course, is to achieve high performance.

When designing for high performance, we work through the OP Model in reverse order from the assessment process. This is depicted in Figure 2–9. The prescription for the design process may be summarized as follows:

1. Define a business strategy that fits the actual business situation facing the organization in the future.
2. Make any needed changes in the design elements to be congruent with the new strategy. This gives structural integrity to the system.
3. Identify the positive and negative impacts the new design elements will have on the culture of the organization.
4. Predict the business results that will be produced by this new culture.

Steps 3 and 4 are merely predictions, of course, but going through the assessment process usually helps managers predict the future developments with more accuracy. Once the new de-

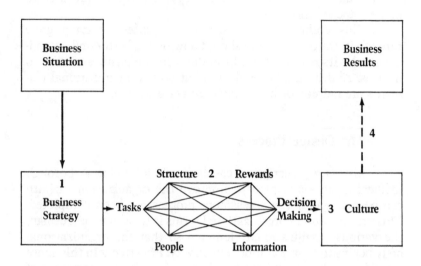

Figure 2–9
The Design Process

sign has been operating for a while, the actual results can be compared to those desired — and the assessment process begins anew.

1. Define a Business Strategy Which Fits the Actual Business Situation

The first step in designing organizations is to engage in strategic planning; that is, exercising strategic choices around what the organization will aim to achieve in the future (see Figure 2–10). In terms of the OP framework, this calls for fitting the business strategy to the business situation that will confront the organization.

A good place to begin is by defining the basic purpose of the organization by asking such questions as: What is our reason for being? What business are we in? How do we choose to compete in our businesses? What are our basic technologies?

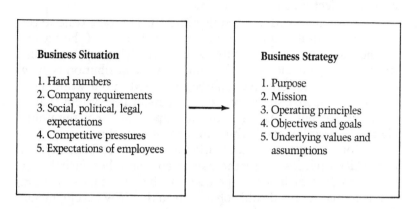

Figure 2–10
Planning the Business Strategy to Fit the Business Situation

As Peter Drucker has said, the answers to these questions are never obvious.[3] I have found this to be very true. If you have any doubts, try the following experiment the next time you convene your management group. Ask each person to give a one-sentence answer to each question above. Start with the first question and go around the table, allowing each person to give an answer. Then move on to the second question, and so forth. I have never found a group that could get beyond the first question without some significant disagreements arising!

I conducted this experiment once with a purchasing department. When asked to define the department's purpose, one manager said matter-of-factly, "Well, that's simple. We are here to purchase materials at the lowest possible price." Almost immediately there was dissension in the ranks. Said a colleague, "Wait a minute! We can't just buy anything that's cheap. The materials have to be of good and reliable quality. We have to purchase based on optimum value, not just the lowest price." Added another, "What about our customers? I have always felt that our primary purpose was to help them meet their volume and profit targets." After a lengthy discussion, the group was able to write a clear, but comprehensive, statement of purpose that had a deeply unifying effect on the whole department.

Many high performing organizations also take time to get a clear sense of mission, or a more personal vision of the future. Mission supplements the purpose by identifying what our distinctive competencies are; what our unique contribution is; how what we want for our lives can be expressed in our work. This is a more personal statement to members of the system than a statement of purpose. Yet both are important for maintaining clarity of direction and high commitment over time.

For example, a manufacturing plant in West Germany had clarified its purpose with the parent company headquarters. It was to produce high quality products at the lowest possible cost. It was to maintain a flexible operation so that new developments could be accommodated quickly and efficiently. It was to avoid labor union or works council confrontations. A similar purpose statement could have applied to every other plant in Europe.

But as the leadership team contemplated the three questions associated with its mission, some powerful energy was unleashed. First, the team recognized its plant had a distinctive technological edge over comparable plants due to size, experience, and organization. Second, it was in a unique position to train new organizations because it was the largest and most experienced plant of its kind in Europe. Third, most members of the leadership team were frustrated by not being the best at what they did. Operational standards had slipped, results were disappointing, and the plant seemed slow to react to new developments. The personal pride of everyone on the team had been hurt.

As the group discussed how it would like to see things in the future, some common threads emerged.

- They would like to be viewed as the technology development center for their products in Europe.
- They would like to be the trainers and standard setters for all future organizations.
- They would like to be the plant that others seek out as a model for running a manufacturing operation.

The phrase, "Be a model for others," was the shorthand way the team members captured this mission statement for themselves.

With this energizing mission in mind, the leadership team went through the remaining steps of the design process and attacked the few key issues that had plagued them in the past. The turnaround in the plant's performance was something to behold. Although there were several plants that fulfilled their basic purpose in the ensuing years, only this one became a model for others in technology development, training, and operational standards. It truly was and continues to be a high performer.

High performers also go a step further by identifying core operating principles. These operating principles are actually statements of core values and desired norms — the deeper elements of culture. These principles become a code of ethics that spell out how the new operation will really operate. By consciously examining these core values and their relevance to the business situation, an organization can do much to position itself for high performance. These statements, when managed effectively, become a new corporate conscience, inviting employees to behave in new ways to support the newly stated purpose or mission. Once people recognize these values are real, they progress even faster toward the desired cultural attributes. This is a common feature of most high performing organizations with which I am acquainted.

The list of the three values that drive the corporate culture in IBM is a good example of impelling operating principles. Everything that is undertaken at IBM is done with these three basic principles in mind:

1. Customer service.
2. Respect for the individual.
3. Excellence in all we do.

Daily decisions, policy formulation, and problem solving are all guided and influenced heavily by these three principles. Those who are familiar with IBM recognize these three characteristics are present wherever "Big Blue" does business.

Similarly, the leaders of a foreign subsidiary of another large multinational corporation were attempting to change their corporate culture to foster high performance. They were frustrated by many telltale signs of a bureaucratic culture — a preoccupation with procedure rather than results, an unhealthy subordination of one's own ideas to the boss's orders, staff groups that were removed from relevant business needs, tunnel vision for one's own needs versus the needs of others, and so on. They identified several operating principles that described what the new culture would look like when the transformation to high performance had been achieved. The following are some of the operating principles they articulated:

1. We will always be one step ahead of our competitors.
2. Each member of the organization will contribute a measurable extra value to our business progress (volume, productivity, and cost effectiveness).
3. We will promote a culture of learning, creativity, change, and action. Everybody's business is identifying opportunities and problems and developing solutions.
4. We will develop commitment to and pride in executable excellence. This will achieve results that allow us to feel proud and enthusiastic about ourselves, our work, and our company.
5. We will strengthen the joint effectiveness between departments and across organizational boundaries and hierarchical levels. "We're all in this together" is the attitude pervading the organization.

When top management introduced these statements in support of the new purpose and mission statements, the reaction from the organization was interesting; most employees had been frustrated by the same cultural characteristics and were glad to see the leaders had finally seen the light. Most importantly, there was now a rallying cry to do business in strongly different ways. The employees enthusiastically accepted the challenge. Management took every possible occasion to reinforce the importance of these operating principles through plant visits, sales force meetings, newsletter articles, and informal discussions. In so doing, they put their principles into action. In time the culture began to move in the desired direction.

With this basic framework of purpose, mission, and operating principles in mind, the organization can then set measurable short-term objectives and goals to round out its business strategy. Once completed, the strategy should be an agreement between the organization and the environment that ensures the goods and services delivered will be valued. This is basic for the ultimate survival of the system. Some helpful questions to be answered as a final check of the strategy are:

- Who is the customer or customers?
- What is our solution to their needs?
- Is our output fit for use by the customer?
- What is our contract (explicit or implicit) with the customer?

2. Make Any Needed Changes in the Design Elements to Fit with the New Strategy

With the new Business Strategy set, we now move to the next step of altering the various Design Elements to be in sync with the new direction (see Figure 2–11). For each strategy chosen, specific tasks will emerge that will have to be designed. Or, as a wise philosopher once said, "At some point, all grand strategies have to degenerate into work!" A strategy that calls for developing breakthrough technologies every five years will require fundamental research tasks to be undertaken that wouldn't be necessary if the strategy were merely to refine the existing tech-

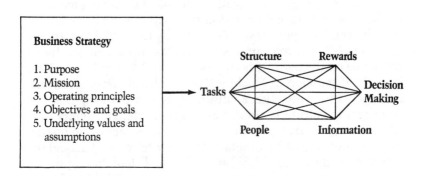

Figure 2–11
Fitting Organizational Design Elements with the Business Strategy

nology. A strategy that identifies employee development as a key competitive thrust will necessitate many tasks to be done (training classes, career planning programs, performance appraisals, etc.) that might otherwise be omitted or handled less comprehensively.

Whatever strategy the organization chooses, there will no doubt be some new tasks that will have to be undertaken and some old tasks that will have to be handled more effectively than in the past. In both situations, some aspects of the current operation will have to be redesigned in order to achieve new performance levels. An interesting exercise after you have completed the business strategy is to list all of the tasks that will have to be done in order to fulfill the strategy. Those who have done this have been surprised at how many tasks emerge on the list. Such a list of tasks is the critical starting point for fitting the design elements to the strategy.

Completing the changes in design elements is a complicated step. The process begins by taking all of the tasks and then developing mechanisms of structure, rewards, decision making, information, and people development to reinforce consistent and long-term high performance of these tasks.

3. Identify the Positive and Negative Impacts the New Design Elements Will Have on the Culture of the Organization

One step that is frequently overlooked is that of predicting the kind of culture and operation that will emerge from the design choices. This prediction is depicted by the dotted-line arrows in Figure 2–12. Given our design choices, what will the likely impact be on the culture, both good and bad? You will remember from the discussion of Machine Theory how design choices can influence an organization's culture. It seems uncanny that the bureaucratic culture is similar everywhere one encounters it — whether it be with governments, school systems, industrial firms, health care units, or retail stores. Once you understand the common design choices that have influenced all of these systems, however, you begin to have an idea of how powerful these choices can be.

One new operation, for instance, was contemplating the

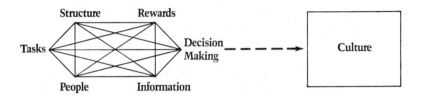

Figure 2–12
Projecting the Cultural Attributes That Will Emerge from Choices About the Design Elements

structure of its pay system. For years, the managers of this new operation had worked in similar departments in which prima donnas had always had a negative impact on the work culture. The prima donnas didn't cooperate well with other employees, always seemed to have their own priorities, or expected preferential treatment. After considerable discussion, it became clear that these prima donnas were usually the highest paid individuals in the department and were the technical specialists. To develop a pay scale with technologists alone at the top of the pyramid would only serve, based on their experience, to perpetuate a similar culture.

So, the group developing the pay structure came up with a radical idea — there would be multiple routes to higher pay. Technologists, team leaders, and those who could work skillfully in all areas of the department all had the same opportunity to rise to the top of the pay scale. This was felt to be more in line with the strong team culture the leaders hoped to establish.

As time went on, their hopes were realized. A strong team culture developed. Technical expertise was comparable with other operations, but the overall flexibility and team spirit had propelled this operation to one division record after another. One of the key ingredients proved to be the multiple routes to the top and an avoidance of stereotyping certain tasks as being better than others.

If one has done a careful assessment to understand the cause-and-effect relationships between culture and current design elements, the chances are high that a future prediction of design elements and culture will be accurate.

4. Predict the Business Results That Will Be Produced by This New Culture

What will be the impact of the new culture on business results, both good and bad? (See Figure 2–13.) Again, the steps taken in the assessment process will prove valuable for this phase of design work. The previous step should have clarified the culture that will emerge. Based on role models within your own system and in other organizations, how will this culture influence the results produced? In retrospect, we can see how culture has powerfully influenced results in a number of arenas.

For instance, in the world of sports, consider the great dynasties of basketball's Boston Celtics and UCLA Bruins; football's Green Bay Packers, Miami Dolphins, and Dallas Cowboys; baseball's New York Yankees. All of these organizations have examples of high performance over long periods of time. Players and/ or coaches were changed during the peak of each of these dynasties, yet the winning continued. Our description for culture in this sports context has usually been team spirit. It is interesting to note that other teams (including the modern version of the

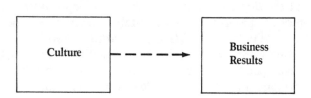

Figure 2–13
Predicting the Business Results That Will Be Delivered by the Way the Organization Really Operates

Yankees) have been unable to duplicate this success regardless of how much money they spent or how many superstars they assembled. A high performing culture cannot be purchased and added to the roster. It exists only to the extent that the individuals in the organization create and sustain it.

In the business world, it is no different. Year after year IBM continues as a high performer in its field. Procter & Gamble continually sets the pace in its consumer products categories. Exxon remains a leader in the oil industry. Each of these companies will tell you that the secret of their consistently high performance is the corporate culture that bonds individuals to the corporate purpose.

Many of the high performing organizations I know have spent considerable effort examining the cultures of high performers in their own systems and in other organizations. After exhaustive study, they are able to reach agreement on the cultural attributes that will be critical for high performance in their given situation.

There are many substeps that accompany each of the four items I have outlined (see Figure 2–14). Chapter 4 elaborates in more detail on each of them. The important thing to be clear about now is that there is a comprehensive framework that can guide both the assessment and design processes.

Conclusion: The Importance of Assessment and Design

There are a few key points I would like to leave with you before going further.

First, the competitive advantage in the technology of Organization Development is the ability to produce true systems change that is enduring. This requires two things:

1. Changing the basic values and assumptions — the core culture — when they are out of sync with business requirements.
2. Structurally reinforcing work behaviors through the de-

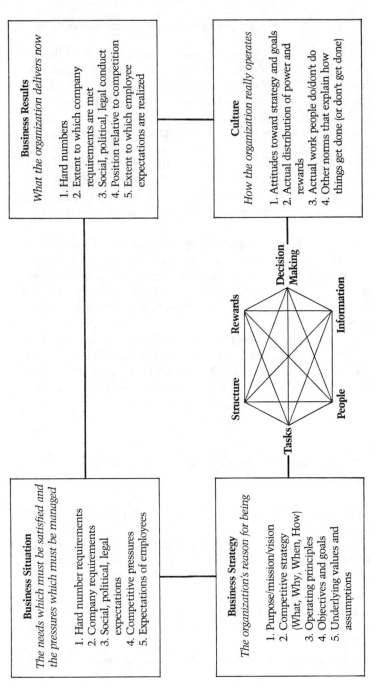

Figure 2-14
Complete Organization Performance Model

sign of the organization to be congruent with the desired strategy.

Producing enduring systems change is an enormous challenge. But then, if it were easy, it would be common to most organizations and would not represent a competitive advantage.

Second, the processes of assessment and design can make a difference in creating and sustaining high performance. These processes not only provide the rational analysis for structural integrity, but also develop commitment (even passion) in the necessary critical mass. It goes without saying that these processes are iterative. High performance isn't something that you launch and then revisit in ten years.

Third, many organizations attempt to assess their effectiveness. The real art is to be able to distinguish critical issues from extraneous ones and to focus on true systems' leverage points rather than hunt for quick-fix solutions. The examples in Chapter 3 should make some of the art of assessment more apparent.

Finally, many organizations understand the need for missions, work teams, pay for contribution, and so on. But few are able to build real understanding and commitment in a critical mass so that assumptions and behaviors are changed. This is the real art of design work. It is largely misunderstood and ignored by managers today. That is why the number of high performers is still relatively small.

All of this presents a big challenge to those working to improve an organization's effectiveness. Creating high performance systems is one of the most difficult undertakings I can think of. It would certainly be easier to issue executive orders, run training seminars, revise policy manuals, and mediate conflicts between bosses and subordinates. Without fitting under the umbrella of a comprehensive organizational change strategy, however, each of these will probably be of little lasting value. If you want to make a difference, learn to manage enduring systems change for high performance. It's risky. It's frustrating. It's often lonely. But it can also be exhilarating and very rewarding. It's like going out on a limb. Sometimes you just have to take the risk, because that's where all the fruit is.

Notes

1. T. E. Deal and A. A. Kennedy, *Corporate cultures* (Reading, Mass.: Addison-Wesley, 1982); A. L. Wilkins, "The culture audit: A tool for understanding organizations," *Organizational Dynamics* (Autumn 1983):24–38; R. R. Thomas, Jr., "Guidelines for identifying organizational culture," unpublished paper, 1983; R. H. Kilmann, *Beyond the quick fix* (San Francisco: Jossey-Bass, 1984); E. H. Schein, *Organizational culture and leadership* (San Francisco: Jossey-Bass, 1985); W. G. Dyer, and W. G. Dyer, Jr., "Organizational development: System change or culture change?" *Personnel*, (February 1986):14–22.

2. J. R. Galbraith, *Organization design* (Reading, Mass.: Addison-Wesley, 1977); D. A. Nadler and M. L. Tushman, "A model for diagnosing organizational behavior," *Organizational Dynamics* (Autumn 1980):35–51.

3. P. F. Drucker, "Business purpose and business mission," in *Management: Tasks, responsibilities, practices* (New York: Harper & Row, 1974), 74–94.

3

The Assessment Process

There are few areas that demonstrate that there is "more than one way to skin a cat" as clearly as the process of assessing the effectiveness of an organization. There are countless ways to measure an organization's performance.

For instance, the questions one asks in an organizational assessment may be tightly structured or open ended. A questionnaire may be designed to gather data, interviews may be conducted, or some combination of both may be used. One may assess performance in respect to some specific issues (e.g., labor relations, flexibility, etc.), or the focus may be on the effectiveness of the total system. David Nadler's book, *Feedback and Organization Development,*[1] is an excellent resource to help the organizational assessor determine which tools will best accomplish what goal.

Marvin Weisbord has summarized some wisdom on the subject of assessment that I have found useful.[2] Recognizing that any assessment is merely a "snapshot" of organizational performance, Weisbord coined what he calls his "First Law of Snapshooting" which is:

"What you look at is what you see."

Some managers are only interested in the bottom line. Others are deeply interested in the effectiveness of work processes in the organization. Specialists are frequently preoccupied with issues that will have an impact on their technology. Whatever your situation may be, you will only be able to assess what you select to examine. This is basic to the principle of information coding covered in Chapter 1. Weisbord also outlined two corollaries to this law: "What you look for is what you find," and "what theory you use determines what you look for."

This chapter focuses only on those approaches to assessment that consider the performance and strategic posture of the total system and uses the OP Model as its theoretical base. The material in this chapter is not meant as a literal blueprint for all specific problems. The precise approach you use will be dependent on your focus and your organization. As Nadler points out in his book, the approach chosen, the level of involvement from others, and the feedback process are all critical factors in conducting a successful assessment. In other words, the assessment process should always be tailored to the organization and its culture in order to have optimal impact.

The OP Framework

When using the OP Model as the framework for assessment, we begin with the business situation and move clockwise through the model. OP maps out the cause-and-effect relationships that lead to overall organizational performance. Therefore, we are concerned not only with issues that emerge in the data collection, but also with what causes them and what effect they have on the rest of the system. There are two questions that may be used as a shorthand way of making these connections in the data. These questions are, "Why?" and "So What?"

For example, if we are interviewing someone about the effectiveness of a scheduling office, that person might say, "People around here always feel like they're in the dark." This information helps us understand the organizational culture and how people feel about working in it. From such responses we may know how people feel, but we do not know how feeling like they're in the dark connects with organizational performance. This is the point at which to pose our two questions. Returning to our interviewee, we might ask, *"Why* do people feel like they're in the dark?" The reply will connect the issue with another part of the system. "It's impossible to schedule meeting rooms. My record of reserved rooms is usually obsolete. The supervisor is always making 'deals' with her friends. I reserve a room only to find out the supervisor scheduled it for a friend without logging it in the record book."

The natural follow-up to such a statement is, "Okay, the supervisor schedules rooms without informing you or logging it in. *So what*? What effect does this have on the scheduling office?" It may be that 15 percent of the scheduling has to be repeated, or 10 percent of the rooms have been booked twice. Employee frustration may be so great that the turnover rate increases. Whatever the situation, the use of the questions allows us to position any piece of data into its proper organizational performance context.

Figure 3–1 represents the steps taken in the above example. The interviewee made a statement about the culture of the organization: people feel they are left in the dark. The follow-up question "Why?" traced the cause back to the design elements (supervisor's decision making and information sharing). The question "So What?" linked the cultural attribute with the results (rework, double booking, or turnover).

There is an important difference between this assessment approach and many traditional organizational sensing processes. If we were merely trying to find out what the major employee concerns were, then we would tabulate their responses to the assessment questions and present the tabulated results to management. Such data, it must be noted, are nothing more than employees' lay perceptions of what needs to be improved. Such perceptions are usually a mixture of symptoms and root causes of systemic problems. They do not help those responsible for the system's performance to have any confidence that addressing the concerns will actually help improve business results. Small wonder that such sensing activities are frequently painful to many managers.

If we are attempting to understand organizational perform-

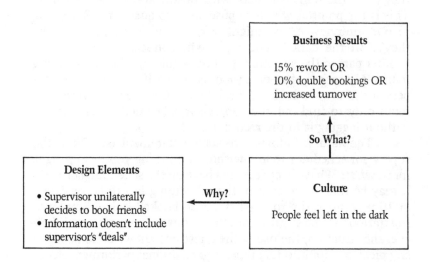

Figure 3–1
Using the Questions "Why?" and "So What?" to Determine Organizational Cause-and-Effect Chains in a Scheduling Office

ance, such data tabulations are not sufficient. Data need to be read within their day-to-day context. We need to connect them with the performance of the total system; to trace their impact on business results. This is not to suggest that employee complaints or issues are not valid in themselves and worthy of management attention. What I am suggesting, however, is that in order to make a real difference in the organization's performance, the issues must be tied into the system's cause-and-effect chains. Only then will there be a meaningful analysis of the organization's present state. Such an analysis is facilitated by using the backtracking methods of the OP Model's assessment process.

I should point out that if one decides to pursue this kind of approach, the interview is a better tool than a questionnaire survey. Personal interaction is required for the interviewee to "make the connections" in the data between causes and effects. In some assessments, we have found it helpful to even organize

Why?	Issue	So What?

Figure 3–2
Sample Assessment Form

our interview sheets to reflect this approach. The interview sheets looked like Figure 3–2. Regardless of what the lead question was, the initial response was noted in the middle column. The follow-up questions were asked and their responses recorded in the appropriate column.

With this framework in mind, let's now consider two typical situations in which it might be used. The first is an organization that wants to assess its performance in the absence of any prior data or measurable targets. The second is an organization that needs a quick snapshot of performance without the luxury of putting together a lengthy and exhaustive study.

SIMI: Assessing a Research Lab

The SIMI research lab employed hundreds of people to develop computer microchips. It was a highly specialized operation that served many customers. SIMI was the symbol of top quality and state-of-the-art technology for years. As competition in Silicon Valley increased sharply in the 1980s, however, SIMI's success in the market began to decline. Competitors' products began to capture many of SIMI's long-time customers.

The lab competed in several different product categories. At the time it was meeting its objectives in roughly 50 percent of them. However, SIMI was not on target in any of its newest categories. Turnover was low, but there were signs that many employees were operating under stress. The competition had developed new products, often preempting SIMI's own years of research work. There was still plenty of business to keep everyone busy for the moment, but the lab manager was anxious to increase the organization's effectiveness in the future.

The organization retained an organizational consultant to help it regain its lost momentum. The lab had no previous experience with formal measures of its performance. Disgruntled employees had written memos through the years to express their frustrations, but a thorough assessment had never been done. The consultant's first recommendation was to conduct an assessment — for the lab to do research on itself. From there, said the expert, management would be able to determine what action to take.

The research manager could not argue against such logic, so the assessment process began. A small study team comprised of internal consultants and line managers was trained in the OP methodology. A random sample of employees at all levels and from each section of the lab was chosen to be interviewed. Interviewers conducted some sessions with individuals and others with small groups. Each interview was structured around three questions.

1. What are your objectives?
2. What helps you achieve these objectives?
3. What prevents you from accomplishing more?

For each response the follow-up questions of "Why?" and "So What?" were asked. This open-ended approach, though very simple in its structure, contained all of the elements necessary for a meaningful assessment of the lab's performance. Note that the words *people* and *organization* were not included anywhere in the three questions. Nonetheless, virtually every answer could be categorized easily into one of the OP Model's five boxes. For example, the first question establishes what the formal and informal business strategies are. The second question serves to identify the actual strengths of the operation — those items that need to be preserved. The final question identifies the basic flaws that need to be corrected in order to achieve high performance.

After weeks of gathering data and diagnosing what they had heard, the study team was able to construct a cause-and-effect chain that explained why the lab's performance had deteriorated.

Culture

SIMI employees described the daily operation as one in which:

- There were first-class facilities, resources, and funds for research.
- Peers had good working relationships and good teamwork.
- People were competent in their assigned work areas.
- Top management supported the lab's reason for being.
- Relationships between bosses and subordinates were generally good.
- There was much stress and pressure applied for short-term results.
- Many felt unrewarded for their efforts or that others were rewarded undeservedly.
- Failure to deliver a project on time was unforgiveable.
- Priorities and objectives were second-guessed by many employees.
- Employees felt they were expected to "do as you're told."
- People were afraid to make a mistake or be associated with a project that failed.
- The company's commitment to its employees had declined (from the employees' view). There was less training and feedback for individual development than in the past.
- Fear and stress sometimes led to attempts to take shortcuts and "beat the system."

Design Elements

The culture was held in place by several structural and procedural norms that had developed in the lab. For example:

- *Decision making* was highly centralized. Most critical decisions were made at the top of the organization and handed down. Frequent reviews were held with top management to examine the progress on a project and to determine what should be done next.
- *Rewards* were generally limited to the formal, visible ones: pay and promotion. There was little informal recognition.
- *Information* was shared fairly well at the higher levels of the system, but the lower levels had little idea of what the business results of the lab were. Information was passed on only to those individuals who needed it for their immediate tasks. The customers, on the other hand, inundated the project leaders with telephone calls and memos, and held frequent meetings to make sure the product would be delivered on time.
- *Structure* divided upstream research from departments working on current products. All employees were organized into natural project teams. Current product team leaders were assigned to work directly with the clients. This often led to a conflict of interests when the client wanted something different from the lab's leadership.
- *People,* especially managers, were rotated from one project to another every two to three years to get a broader sense of the business. All of the lab's top managers had worked in more than one product category. Hourly employees were capable individuals hired from the local area. Managers were recruited from many of the nation's top universities. The younger managers entered the organization anxious to prove themselves to upper management and move ahead in the system.
- The research *task* process was tedious, uncertain, and it often took years to see final results. Personal vision, technical competence, absolute integrity, tenacity, and coor-

dinated action planning were all critical elements of successful research work.

Business Strategy

The assessment process discovered a wide gap between the formal business strategy and the actual operating strategy. For instance:

- The formal strategy was to develop robust technology that would beat competition's offerings in every category. A technical edge was seen as the lab's only way to command customer loyalty. Short-term pressures were to be ignored if they required the erosion of this technical edge.
- People in the system responded that their objectives were primarily threefold: (1) to contribute to the lab's short-term volume and profit goals; (2) move their projects ahead; and (3) improve and apply technology. This focus was noticeably more short-term than the formal one.

Let's use the OP Model to summarize what was happening in the SIMI organization in the specific areas of successful new category introductions and maintaining a technology edge over the competition. Both results were off target. (See Figure 3–3.)

Entries into new categories had been made at an accelerated pace, but few of them had been successful. Customers thought that most of SIMI's new products were average in terms of technology. Management's question was, "Why?" The culture data provided some clues.

Employees felt incredible stress and pressure to deliver their project on time. Because management made most of the major decisions, those actually working on the projects came to believe they were merely small cogs in a giant machine. Middle management's commitment to the product's success had declined drastically. So, most people focused on getting the project completed on time and hoped to move to a new assignment before the final results became clear. This certainly was not the kind of culture that would produce large technological advan-

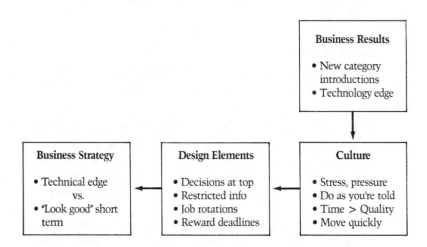

Figure 3-3
OP Model Assessment of SIMI Results in Two Areas

tages. "Why?" management asked. The design elements helped answer this query.

By maintaining tight controls over decisions and information, the top management had made it very difficult for its subordinates to feel as though they had any creative control and consequently felt as if they were not important, vital contributors to the life of the lab. These two design elements also fueled the stress and pressure that one felt; there were many critical unknowns. The elements of two to three year assignment changes and rewards for meeting deadlines had led to the dynamics of valuing completion time over product quality. The frequent moves also served further to reduce the feelings of commitment to what one was doing. Small wonder the culture had evolved into one in which everyone was working to get the job out on time.

"How could such a thing happen?" management asked. They believed they had spent considerable time declaring what the strategy was for the lab and what was needed to produce a technical edge. The responses to the study question, "What are your objectives?" provided the final piece of the puzzle.

Although the formal strategy was to develop a competitive technical edge, most employees had only short-term targets in mind as they went about their daily work. Those working on current products were bombarded by demands from customers (from whom they got a lot of input). In the absence of comparable information from lab management, project teams gradually started focusing on short-term results. Coupled with the high need most young managers had to show results and move up in the system, the common operational strategy was to look good short-term. Unknowingly, the system of design elements had nourished this operational strategy by the way it controlled, rewarded, and organized its human resources.

Based on this assessment, SIMI managers were able to rethink their approach to the business. Much attention was given to reinforcing the lab's basic strategy to all employees. The job rotation was slowed down considerably. Efforts to increase personal ownership were initiated through leadership conferences and daily coaching. "Do as you're told" was driven out by consistent encouragement by top management to "push back." In time the SIMI culture started to become more suited for high performance.

National Computer: Assessing Late Customer Payments

The National Computer Company (NACOM) was a relatively young computer firm located in the Northeast. It soon gained a reputation for high quality and dependable personal computers, and was now one of the market leaders in its category. Success had brought its own set of problems, however. Sales were booming, but the administrative system at NACOM was having trouble keeping up with the sales volume.

Every time a sales representative sold a NACOM computer to a customer, an order form was filled out and sent into the division office to be processed. Based on the information on the order form, equipment would be packaged and shipped, an invoice would be sent to the customer, and internal auditing would make adjustments in the inventory and accounting systems. A nagging problem was the rate at which customers actually paid for their merchandise. The Accounts Receivable (AR) account (e.g., payments that were due but not yet collected) was growing at an alarming rate. In the last fiscal year, for example, sales revenues had increased 10 percent, but delinquent payments had increased 100 percent!

AR was a major problem for the entire industry. The industry average was ninety days, meaning it took nearly three months to collect payment after the equipment was received by the customer. NACOM's AR average was sixty days. Not only did this represent millions of delayed (and lost interest) dollars, but NACOM had been steadily increasing staff resources to account for and track down the late payments. The total overhead expenses to track AR were several million dollars each year and still growing! Now management was considering a sophisticated computer tracking system to improve the control of AR. NACOM retained a consulting firm to gather some data and recommend precisely what should be done to reduce AR to one half of its present level.

The consultants conducted interviews in a few divisions where AR levels represented the lowest, the average, and the highest in the company. Using a framework similar to the OP Model, they soon had a comprehensive picture of the AR situation. The consultants met just a few days before they would make a presentation to the sponsoring division's vice president. Somehow they needed to consolidate all of their information and present it in a form that would be familiar and understandable to the vice president. To do this, they employed a tool known as the *Organization Performance Review.*

The Organization Performance Review is a simplified version of the OP Model. If the OP Model is like a mainframe computer, the Performance Review is like a manager's pocket calculator. In OP Model terms, this review probes into the causes and effects of organizational performance by asking some fundamental questions related to culture, design elements, and strategy. Each question asks the evaluator to compare what is happening in the organization today with ideal results and culture behaviors. Because the questions also correspond to the business strategy and each of the design elements, they guide one through the critical cause/effect linkages in the system. This tool has certain advantages over the full OP Model approach:

- It facilitates looking at the whole system for preliminary analyses.
- It is helpful in making a review when time is short.
- It works effectively with others who may not be familiar with the OP Model.

However, one should not expect the Performance Review's outcome to be as comprehensive as the OP Model approach. It does not illustrate the interdependency of the various elements, nor does it show the cause-and-effect chains as clearly.

Here's how the Organization Performance Review works. For any results area (profitability, customer service, quality measures, employee satisfaction, etc.) answer these questions:

1. Is the *result* satisfactory?
2. Which *cultural* values, assumptions, and behaviors critically influence the results?
3. Do *decisions* reflect knowledge, experience, and a bias for action?
4. Are desired behaviors *rewarded* or punished? Are undesired behaviors *rewarded* or punished?
5. Is the needed *information* available?
6. Does the *structure* permit the right people to work together on the tasks?
7. Do *people* have the skills to do the tasks?
8. Are specific *tasks* clearly identified that will lead to achieving the strategy and goals?
9. Do the *strategy* and goals ensure a competitive advantage; are they clear?; and do they have the commitment of key players?

For each question, a simple yes or no is only the beginning. From there, the data observed or collected should be noted. Each major subsystem should be reviewed under each question area when appropriate. The questions "Why?" and "So What?" can be helpful here as well. The result is a framework that lends itself to a reasonably comprehensive assessment without requiring an exhaustive process. Some groups have been able to produce a very revealing summary of their organization's performance in a few hours.

Now let's see how this consulting firm employed the Organization Performance Review to assess NACOM's AR situation. Pages and pages of interview notes and handouts were discussed and key themes were grouped under each of the nine questions. In only a couple of days, the complex NACOM system was exposed as follows:

1. *Is the result satisfactory?* The answer was obviously no. AR levels were at sixty days; management wanted it reduced to an average of thirty days. This improvement would put millions of dollars into the corporate coffers to be used at the company's discretion. As it was, the money was tied up and unavailable for company use.

2. *Which cultural values, assumptions, and behaviors critically influence the results?* NACOM's culture represented positive and negative forces that influenced the AR result. There was a strong value placed on improving how work was done. And NACOM employees wanted to be the best in their business. Hard work and extensive problem analysis were norms. There was pride in meeting objectives. All of these factors made the consultants believe that the problem could be corrected.

But there were some cultural obstacles that up to now had been stronger than the positive factors. There was still a start-up mentality in the new company; employees were used to doing what needed to be done without worrying about costs or cash flow. The sales representatives, those who were closest to the customer and who were in the best position to influence AR on the front end, were minimally involved in NACOM's AR improvement effort.

These sales reps held somewhat exalted positions in the company and often felt above accounting problems. Line management gave orders on the really "important" matters; the initiative for AR seemed to come from a headquarters staff group.

3. *Do decisions reflect knowledge, experience, and a bias for action?* Although there was a bias for action at NACOM, few of the critical decisions reflected the most knowledge and experience the company had to put against the issue. Targets were established at headquarters, not by those who were closest to the customer. The AR department was attempting to change accounting procedures and control mechanisms, yet the people in the field were the most familiar with what went on in the daily business.

4. *Are the desired behaviors rewarded or punished?* Are undesired behaviors rewarded or punished? There were many reward mechanisms in NACOM, but very few of them had anything to do with improving AR. Senior management bonuses were influenced only to a small degree by AR performance. Up until now, no general manager had been punished for failure to improve AR levels. The sales representatives were not rewarded for accuracy at the front end; in fact, they were rewarded on the basis of quick sales, customer relations, and sales volume. As previously noted, the culture also reinforced the actual current dynamics: Sales reps were supposedly too important to worry about what they considered the petty details of billing. AR had received very little attention outside of those within the department. Members of this department were rewarded for accuracy in their work and for quick AR turnaround.

5. *Is the needed information available?* There were several key feedback loops that were not functioning well. Few of NACOM's employees knew why the people at headquarters were getting so excited about AR. The sales representatives failed to pass on much critical information and never heard about the errors they made at billing or on the systemwide repercussions these errors caused. A central billing group controlled the invoice processing system, but employees in the field were not informed when the invoices would be received by cus-

tomers to start up the AR procedures. In an effort to reduce confusion over multiple targets (there were eleven different measurements that related to AR), some divisions refused to pass them on to the field.

6. *Does the structure permit the right people to work together on the tasks?* Clearly, the sales representatives were not working together effectively with the rest of the system. Their mistakes multiplied in severity as they moved through the system. The headquarters and field offices were not working together optimally. As noted previously, they had different targets and each did what they felt was called for, given their objectives. The headquarters group in charge of setting targets was not in tune with many realities of daily life in the field. The field offices spent much time second-guessing the quotas handed down from headquarters. The department established to focus single-mindedly on AR was getting little cooperation from the other key departments. No one else was as concerned with AR levels as they were.

7. *Do people have the skills to do the tasks?* Generally speaking, NACOM had a highly skilled work force. People had the required skills to do their jobs. The only exception to this was the AR group, where assignments lasted anywhere from sixty days to six months. These short assignments simply did not allow the group to understand the system or build enough continuity to be an effective factor in controlling AR.

8. *Are specific tasks clearly identified that will lead to achieving the strategy and goals?* Each of the eleven targets was the result of a complicated mathematical calculation. Consequently, the targets were not widely understood by all members of the system. This made it difficult for people to focus on specific tasks to reach the targets. Upon further examination of the administrative system that resulted in AR, the assessors learned that many of the customers' late payments were due to incorrect shipments or inadequate information on the invoice! Customers had to return merchandise or invoices to NACOM and wait for the corrections to be

made before paying. In most cases, the sales representative failed to document the correct information at the time of the sale. The rest of the system wrestled with considerable time and expense to compensate for these errors at the front end. Another issue was the conflict of corporate credit policies with the AR goal. NACOM had a policy of allowing government agencies and preferred customers sixty days or more before payment was due. How was one to enforce a thirty-day AR target with these accounts?

9. *Do the strategy and goals ensure a competitive advantage; are they clear; and do they have the commitment of the key players?* The assessors found that NACOM's goals relating to AR were neither clear nor committed to by many key players and departments. There were eleven different measures for AR, each relevant for some parts of the organization, but not for others. For instance, the division president's bonus was calculated in part by the division's twelve-month cumulative delinquent rate (of which AR was only one of many factors). Field offices used a separate measure to approximate what they could influence of the total delinquent rate. Regional and branch managers received their bonuses based on a third measure of delinquent payments. In all cases, it was possible to improve the total figure while making minimal progress on AR.

The targets themselves were established at division headquarters and passed on to the field. Each local office felt their targets were unreasonable in some areas and spent considerable time lobbying to have the numbers revised. When unsuccessful in this effort, they did the best they could and then at the end of the fiscal year presented the factors that had prevented achievement of the goals.

Remember, NACOM's management was on the brink of installing a sophisticated computer tracking system to improve AR results before the consultants were brought in! This would have been similar to prescribing training as the panacea for any individual performance shortfalls — regardless of what those shortfalls were!

The consultants presented their assessment data to the division vice president. The presentation was a simple flow of the causes and effects in the system that yielded the current AR results. The vice president was impressed and agreed with the consultants that some fundamental changes in the existing system were called for before installing any more personnel or systems to correct the AR problem. NACOM began to pursue these systems improvements with the help of the consultants.

Using Assessment Data to Improve Performance

Hopefully, the case examples of SIMI and NACOM have demonstrated how one might assess organizational performance. But remember, the art of assessment is to distinguish critical issues from extraneous ones and focus on true systems leverage points rather than quick fix solutions. The OP Model can give us tips on the mechanics, but what about the art?

To answer this question, let's look at all of the steps involved in assessing a large, complex organization:

1. *Data collection* — using the OP Model, Organization Performance Review, or similar tools.
2. *Analysis* — examining the data to determine the major themes. This process begins by breaking the data into natural topics. Within each topic, the major themes are extrapolated from the data. These themes are the essence of what the people said, both good and bad. Demographic profiles are often helpful in developing themes.
3. *Synthesis* — putting the pieces together to form an overall impression. Synthesis includes determining the relative importance and energy around each topic. The level of intensity is an important consideration for the whole system, for example, "The pay could be better, but I'm satisfied for now," or "If I don't get more money soon,

I'm gonna quit!" The difference between these two themes (both of which could be labeled *pay concerns*) is significant. This phase should also produce an accurate reflection of the total system, that is, "The system looks very good;" "The system is in deep trouble;" or "The system is doing okay for now, but there are storm clouds on the horizon."

4. *Hypothesis* — using organization theory, experience, or understanding to conceptualize what is happening in the organization and answer the questions "Why?" and "So What?" The models in this book have all proven to be helpful in answering these two questions. The challenge is for one to explain causes and effects at the total system level. Effects (results) come from so many interrelated causes that identifying an accurate map can seem overwhelming.

5. *Action plan* — determining the key priorities to improve organizational performance. If the assessment data have been accurately collected, analyzed, and synthesized, one should have a good understanding of those few areas where changes or interventions would make a difference in the total organization's performance.

Many organizations are able to collect and analyze data skillfully. The real art (and the crucial factor in developing effective change interventions) is to synthesize, hypothesize, and create effective action plans. If the whole is greater than the sum of the parts, as Open Systems Theory tells us, then even superb analysis of the pieces is not enough. The pieces must be synthesized to give us an accurate understanding of the whole; and our hypotheses and action plans must be based on this understanding.

The key to effective action is to determine where the leverage points are. Leverage points are those few factors that will have a major impact on the entire system. To state it in terms of Pareto's Law, leverage points represent 20 percent of all possible actions that will lead to 80 percent of the improvements in the total system.

Identifying Leverage Points

The first essential step in identifying leverage points is to remember what it is we are trying to leverage — the performance (behaviors) of individuals across the system that directly influences the results. In terms of the OP Model, this would require that we carefully examine the business results and culture boxes. What specific behaviors need to be changed? Perhaps some current practices need to be modified or stopped. Or it may be that some critical behaviors are not evident. In any event, the current level of organizational performance is the result of things people are doing or not doing. Let's synthesize the examples of SIMI and NACOM separately and find the leverage points.

SIMI's top management stepped back from the pages of assessment data and attempted to view the data more holistically. "What is this information telling us?" they asked. When they distilled their information, what most concerned them was that SIMI's technical innovation (especially in new product lines) was not competitive. After studying the assessment data, they traced this problem to three aspects of cultural behavior:

- Overly submissive behaviors. ("Do as you're told.")
- Conservative behaviors. ("Don't make a mistake.")
- Shortcut behaviors. ("Beat the system.")

The leaders attempted to synthesize the message from these three types of behaviors:

- We all don't have the same strategy.
- We all don't feel like owners of the business.
- We all aren't demonstrating the leadership required for innovation and growth.

By examining the design elements and business strategy areas, a few key leverage points emerged that were unified into an action plan.

- *Business Strategy:* the firm's basic business strategy was shared more deeply and personally with the aim of creating ownership for it by virtually every employee.

- *Structure:* ownership was also increased by slowing down the job rotation and increasing the link between personal success and business results.
- *People:* an intensive leadership conference was organized for the key levels of top and middle management. These conferences reinforced the need for cultural change and gave the participants the opportunity to reevaluate their own roles in and responsibilities for shaping the culture.

Because each of these three action steps was integral to the existing cause-and-effect chain in SIMI, the total culture began to shift in the desired direction. The culture had taken years to digress to the point when the assessment was undertaken. After eighteen months of implementing the action plan the progress was slow, but steady. Management was encouraged that a new culture was being established that would yield the desired business results.

NACOM provides another example of what happens when leverage points are identified and used to plan change. A synthesis of NACOM's situation indicated that:

- Goals were unclear.
- The sales reps were only minimally involved in improvement of AR (structure) even though they were the critical resources at the front end of the system.
- There were several loopholes in the information and tracking systems.
- There was little reward or punishment for meeting AR expectations.

The leverage points appeared obvious when analyzing the situation with the OP Model. NACOM went to work on each one with real determination.

- The eleven AR measures were reduced to five, providing more focus and common ownership to work on the problem.
- Cross-functional teams were formed (including sales reps) to work with each customer group. The mission of these teams was to improve customer service — and so reduce AR.

- A series of workshops was held to analyze the AR work flow through the entire system. Representatives of all corporate disciplines participated in identifying loopholes, redundancies, and inefficiencies. They also designed improvements to the system that paid off very quickly.
- The rewards system was affected in several ways. The changes in measurements and the workshops highlighted how serious the AR situation was. The sales reps' bonus plan was also modified to include points for reducing AR.

All of these changes proceeded simultaneously. The results were dramatic. At the end of twelve months, the thirty-day target was being met in many departments and the total revenue tied up in AR was only 50 percent of what it had been!

Conclusion

The assessment process is critical to creating High Performance Organizations. It is the diagnosis that must precede prescription if the root causes of the ailment are to be treated. Complex organizations have thousands of symptoms that might divert the manager's time and attention. Assessment acts as a safeguard and allows the organization to know that the few things it chooses to initiate will lead to meaningful performance gains in the entire organization. It is often tempting to make a snap assessment of the current situation and immediately prescribe actions that will improve things. Too often these prescriptions treat only the symptoms.

The tools outlined in this chapter can help the manager distinguish true root causes and leverage points for influencing them. Effective assessment requires discipline more than it requires time. Tools like the ones described here allow their users the ability to inject this needed discipline into the assessment process. Regardless of the size of the organization seeking improvement, its capacity for managing change will be limited by the press of the daily business activities. These tools can identify the critical 20 percent of the activities that will bring the 80 percent improvement for the system.

Once the assessment is complete, the next task is to plan, or design, the improvements that will lead to high performance. This process for designing is the subject of Chapter 4.

Notes

1. D. A. Nadler, *Feedback and organization development: Using data-based methods* (Reading, Mass.: Addison-Wesley, 1977).
2. M. R. Weisbord, "The two first laws of diagnosis and action," unpublished paper.

4

The Design Process

The notion that one can actually shape the ways a large organization does its work is indeed a staggering one! Ironically, most managers are unaware that they actually do this every day. As I said earlier, every aspect of organizational behavior is designed — one way or another. Too frequently it is done unconsciously and without an insistence that the design choice be consistent with the organization's strategy. But organizations are shaped, designed, and redesigned all the time.

Alternately, designing organizations for high performance is a relatively rare occurrence. As in many other critical organizational endeavors, excellence in design execution requires observance of some fundamental principles of human behavior and a comprehensive business perspective. This chapter presents the theoretical background and some approaches that have been used successfully to design large organizations for high performance.

What happens in an effective organizational design process? There are many steps to be covered, but for now, try to think of the design process as a few critical activities:

1. Negotiating a contract (purpose) for goods and services with the environment.

2. Balancing the organization's resources to accomplish all of the needed tasks with excellence.
3. Reinforcing and maintaining this high performance over time.
4. Renegotiating the contract as environmental needs change.

This design process is an iterative one. When one considers the short-term adjustments that may be required because something isn't going quite right in addition to the renegotiation process, it is safe to say that design work is really never done. The process of designing organizations is crucial. Through it you can literally create the kind of organization (and high performance) you want to have.

The technology of organization design has emerged from classical strategic planning and experiences gained in work design over the past forty years.[1] I will not attempt to give a rundown of all the possible technologies that one could use. Because of our exposure to Open Systems Theory, however, I would like briefly to review two technologies that have their roots in Systems Theory. These technologies are Sociotechnical Systems Design and Open Systems Planning. Both have had a major influence on many of the high performing systems that I have seen.

Sociotechnical Systems

In the early 1950s a group of behavioral scientists from London's Tavistock Institute of Human Relations headed by Fred Emery and Eric Trist conducted some work experiments with coal mine operators in South Yorkshire, England.[2] Emery and Trist were trying to see what effect differing work structures would have on productivity and overall effectiveness. One of their beliefs was that business results were influenced heavily by both social factors (interactions, support, supervision, etc.) and technical factors (equipment, materials, etc.).

The Tavistock group altered the work arrangements in different groups while keeping their technical factors constant. Conventional coal mining methods were designed according to Ma-

Table 4-1

*Productivity and Costs for Different Forms of Work
Organization with Same Technology*

	Conventional	Sociotechnical
Production efficiency (%)	78	95
Overtime (hours/shift)	1.32	0.03
Turnover (% of total work force)	6	0
% Shifts with cycle lag	69	5
No. of consecutive weeks without losing a cycle	12	65

chine Theory principles and called for each miner to do only a single, partial task with little or no social interaction. The method proposed by the Tavistock group had each miner do a variety of tasks in cooperation with different members of a relatively autonomous work group. These work groups interchanged roles and shifts and regulated their affairs with a minimum of supervision. In analyzing the outcomes of the conventional and sociotechnical systems (STS), it became clear that the latter produced far superior results[3] (see Table 4–1).

The sociotechnical structure also proved to be superior in the area of stress indicators[4] as seen in Table 4–2.

It is interesting to note that the miners reported the new sociotechnical work organization was based on practices com-

Table 4-2

Stress Indices for Different Social Systems

	Conventional	Sociotechnical
Absenteeism without reason (% of possible shifts)	4.3	0.4
Sickness or other	8.9	4.6
Accidents	6.8	3.2
Total	20.0	8.2

mon in unmechanized days (e.g., before Machine Theory!) when small groups took responsibility for the entire cycle and worked autonomously. These initial results were most encouraging and led to other experiments in STS work design. Subsequent results have been consistent with these initial findings even though the systems that tried STS have been located all over the world and have included such diverse situations as coal mining operations, oil refineries, office operations, auto assembly lines, consumer goods manufacturing, health care units, religious organizations, civil service agencies, and financial organizations.[5]

The key principles of STS that have contributed to our understanding of effective work design may be summarized as follows:[6]

1. Overall productivity is directly related to the system's accurate analysis of social and technical needs and requirements. This substantiates Open Systems Theory's premise that the output is achieved through balancing the task, group, and individual core processes.
2. An accurate analysis of the social and technical needs usually leads to work designs with the following characteristics:

    - *Minimal critical specification of rules* — This principle has two aspects, negative and positive. The negative simply states that no more should be specified than is absolutely essential; the positive requires that we identify what is critical to overall success. In practice this means the work design should be precise about what has to be done, but not how to do it. The use of rules, policies, and predefined procedures is kept to the absolute minimum.
    - *Variance control* — Variances, or deviations from the ideal process, should be controlled at the point where they originate. This recognizes each individual as the first line of defense for his or her respective core tasks and the manager as the first line of defense for most boundary-related tasks.
    - *Multiskills* — Each member of the system should be skilled in more than one function so that the work

system becomes more flexible and adaptive. This allows a function to be performed in many ways utilizing different people.

* *Boundary location* — Roles that are interdependent should be within the same departmental boundaries. Interdependence may be a function of both knowledge and expertise. Boundaries are usually drawn on the basis of one or more of three criteria: technology, territory, or time. Boundaries based on technology group departments by function (marketing/manufacturing; operations/warehouse; ordering/customer relations) or by product line. Boundaries based on territory group departments by proximity of resources (country subsidiaries; Plant A; Northeast Sales Division). Boundaries based on time group departments by schedule or event (first, second, or third shift; fall sales campaign team; winter road crew).

* *Information flow* — Information systems should be designed primarily to provide information to the point of action and problem solving. This is in contrast to most systems, which provide information based on hierarchical channels. For instance, policy changes in calculating finance charges should go directly to the clerks doing these calculations, not only to their supervisors.

* *Support congruence* — The social system should be designed to reinforce the behaviors intended by the new structure. Rewards, hiring practices, departmental structures, training systems, and so on all need to be congruent with the basic work design and work group structures. For example, it would be incongruent to reward narrow skill specialization if one were striving for multiskills.

* *Design and human values* — The design should achieve high results by providing a high quality of work life to fulfill individual needs. This is the very heart of STS theory. Superior results come from the joint optimization of individual and organizational needs.

Note how these principles of work design reinforce and act with some of the natural characteristics of living systems outlined in Chapter 1. Collectively they spell out how one goes about balancing the core processes to improve the output. They also increase the system's ability to be self-regulating by creating work groups with a *clear sense of purpose* (e.g., critical specification), *inputs and feedback* (variance control and information to the point of action), *capability for self-sufficiency* (multiskills and boundary location), and *meeting individual needs* (design and human values).

The specific techniques of how one actually designs work based on these principles is covered in detail in Chapter 5. Ever since the initial experiments in the British coal mines, these principles have been tried in an environment dominated by Machine Theory. Skeptics have abounded. Successes have been discounted by some through the years. These tendencies to preserve the steady state should be recognizable in light of our discussion of Open Systems Theory. But the record is quite conclusive: work organizations patterned after these principles have improved business results and increased individual commitment and motivation.

Open Systems Planning

Sociotechnical design proved to be quite successful in organizing work around the core process to yield better results. Unfortunately, this did not always prove to be sufficient to keep the enterprise afloat. As we learned earlier, the effects of a changing environment on an organization's core process can be critical. Working optimally on the core process will not guarantee survival if its output is no longer valued by the environment.

In the late 1960s a small team of consultants led by James Clark, Charles Krone, G. K. Jayaram, and Will McWhinney developed a technology for addressing the interface between organization and the environment.[7] Their technology became known as *Open Systems Planning* (OSP). It was the first attempt to help organizations methodically analyze the environmental demands and expectations placed on them and plan to successfully meet these demands and expectations. As with Sociotechnical Systems, the variations in applying OSP are almost endless. Most approaches that I have seen utilize the following core elements:

1. Scanning the Environment — Defining the Present Situation is done in terms of expectations and interactions between the external domains of the environment and the organization itself. (See Figure 4–1.)

    The planners identify the key groups in the organization's environment and answer the following questions:

    • What do they expect of us? What do we expect of them?
    • How do they interact with us? How do we interact with them?
    • How do they affect our results? How do we affect theirs?

2. Predicting the Realistic Future Environmental Situation — is an extension of the present assuming that no deliberate intervention for change occurs. The planning group assesses the proposition, "If nothing else changes, what will the future look like if the present situation continues for the next N years?"

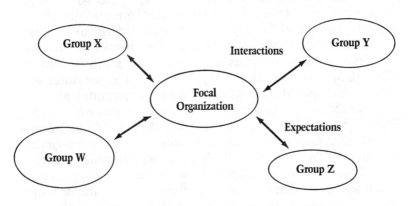

Figure 4–1
A Map Illustrating an Environmental Scan

3. Defining the Ideal Future Situation — assumes that the planning group can intervene and change any aspect of the present situation. By changing what is undesirable, what impact would this have on the future situation? The planning group considers the following:

   • What would it look like if Group X were interacting effectively with us?
   • What would Group Y's ideal expectations be of us?
   • What would it look like if we were interacting effectively with Group Z?
   • What would be our desired expectations of Groups W, X, Y, and Z?

4. Action Planning — identifies specific steps to create the ideal future situation. As outlined in Chapter 1, such steps usually fall into one of the following categories:

   • Changing the influences and functions of some external groups. How could we cause Group X to interact differently with us?
   • Changing your own operations in response to critical outside requirements. How should we be interacting differently with Group Z?
   • Changing the relationship and transactions with outside groups by mutually redefining expectations, workloads, and purposes. How could we influence Group Y to change its expectations of us? Which of our expectations of Groups W, X, Y, and Z do we need to modify?

Many organizations have used variations of OSP techniques to handle their environmental interfaces more skillfully. This is a good example of how practical techniques can demystify a theoretical notion like *managing the environment*.

Previous Applications of OSP and STS: A Commentary

Many managers and consultants were quick to see the advantages of combining the technologies of STS and OSP into one design process. OSP provided a means to negotiate the contract, or purpose, with the environment, while STS allowed managers to balance the critical transformation processes to fulfill the purpose. Many of the High Performance Organizations described in the literature have used some combination of these two technologies to help them achieve their results. However, these new theories have not been applied without their own set of unintended consequences. Along with better efficiency, productivity, employee motivation, and satisfaction have come some undesirable outputs. These unwanted side effects have resulted mostly from assumptions and practices which have fallen short of the theoretical underpinnings. Ord Elliott has very capably identified some of the most common problems experienced to date by those implementing STS and OSP.[8]

1. The personal satisfaction with skill development and career progress tends to peak out over time. Individual work roles in STS/OSP organizations are typically *enlarged* (more variety of tasks) and *enriched* (more discretion and autonomy) over roles designed by Machine Theory. At first, there is great excitement and motivation produced by these new work roles. In time, however, people desire even greater challenge and autonomy. This usually occurs within five to eight years of the new organization design's introduction. Unless further improvements are made, even the innovative work culture begins to struggle like its predecessors (though in relatively milder proportions) with boredom, decreased trust in management, and the "just put in your time" syndrome.

2. The management organization structure and rewards system has remained basically unaltered despite major changes in other employee work and rewards systems. At some point the two systems become incompatible and the management system becomes a limiting factor to further development of individuals and work groups. There are two classes of citizens: managers and non-managers.

3. First-level managers are caught in the squeeze between

the two systems. They become frustrated and unsure of their future as they walk the tightrope between management and nonmanagement.

4. There are compatibility issues between the innovative organizations using STS/OSP practices and environmental groups. The culture and norms may vary greatly, causing tension at the interface. Quality attention to the ongoing interfaces between the organization and outside groups has been inadequate in most cases.

5. Even the innovative organizations have not always proven to be flexible enough when the business curve flattens or declines. Phenomena such as the fluctuations in the computer industry in the 1980s challenge our known capability to respond to environmental changes.

6. The business rationale for such organizational experiments has been blurred in some cases to the point that it has been neglected. Energy and drive to make the system operate as intended sometimes outweigh the energy and drive to deliver the needed business results, especially in times of crisis.

These six problems have plagued many innovative organizations in the past thirty years. More recently the literature has been helpful in documenting how these issues have curtailed organizational performance.[9] But there has been little published on what to do about them. Why have they arisen and what could be done to remedy them?

The Common Plague: Internal Myopia

In retrospect, it appears that few organizations have been able to escape the obsession of focusing too heavily on their internal operations and ignoring important signals from their environment. The term I use to describe this obsession is *Internal Myopia*. Open Systems approaches, theoretically, should be able to help organizations overcome such tendencies. Unfortunately, most Open Systems approaches have been treated as exercises rather than principles for managing an enterprise. Once the exercise has been completed, the attention has turned to (and remained fixed on) improving internal efficiencies. Certainly this pattern has been a disappointment both to the originators of the models and to the organizations who expected better results to flow from the so-called completion of the exercise.

I believe this difficulty has arisen, in part, because of the underlying assumption of the organizational planners that "we know best" and the way this assumption has caused organization design technology to be applied to date. These two factors have prevented many going through OSP from *really listening* to the signals in their environment. Consequently, each of the six chronic problems associated with Internal Myopia may be traced to the tendency of the system to focus almost exclusively on its task core process. A critical challenge to the organization designer, therefore, is to overcome this strong (and understandable) preoccupation with self. When unrestrained, Internal Myopia causes organizations to gradually drift out of touch with their environments.

This Internal Myopia also causes one of the great paradoxes of our age — the situation in which businesses are constantly waging battle for survival in volatile environments, while many of their employees and subsystems are facing the syndrome of peaking out. How can this occur? Answering this question unlocks the riddle of the paradox.

Some parts of an organization may peak out while the total system is fighting for its life because *each part is focused on a narrow, relatively static set of business parameters.* According to contemporary organizational practice, manufacturing should concern itself only with production and quality control. Marketing should concern itself only with addressing consumer needs. Research and development should concern itself only with developing the product. Sales should concern itself only with trade relations.

Oversimplified? Yes. A reflection of typical real-life corporate thinking? Yes! Once we come to grips with the reality of this situation, two points become clear:

1. This is a problem of organization design — corporate resources are frequently being applied against too few tasks.

2. This explains why past Open Systems Planning and Sociotechnical Systems approaches have had little influence outside their own departmental laboratories. Most organizations that have applied these technologies in the past have taken as a given the strong departmental boundaries imposed upon them by the larger corporation.

Thus, while these innovative organizations preached "ever increasing contribution and effectiveness," they *practiced* "but only against a finite set of responsibilities." The peaking out is an inevitable consequence of such incongruence. Remember, Systems Theory teaches us to expect suboptimization of the whole if only one part is optimized.

If we return for a moment to the world of small family businesses, we find a different set of dynamics. Each member feels like an owner in the business. You won't hear the phrase, "That's not my job!" from anyone. Typically, these organizations operate with leaner staffing levels and a deeper sense of commitment than what is found in today's larger organizations. Peaking out is seldom seen because each person is focused on the success of the total enterprise and is in a position to influence any needed task. More than ever before, these same dynamics are needed in large organizations.

For example, manufacturing is certainly in a position to spot problems and opportunities in the areas of raw material specifications, distribution, engineering technology, and quality evaluations, to name only a few. Similarly, purchasing and sales are in a position to observe new developments among competitors and the wholesale trade that may be crucial inputs to marketing. Similar examples may be found for virtually every functional subgroup. Ask yourself the question, "If this were my business, would I get involved with other departments to improve things?" The answer most probably would be yes. Yet, the way most organizations are currently designed, few leaders expect broader involvement in the business from specific departments.

The Outside-In Approach:
True Open Systems Designing

There is a new approach to designing organizations that I have found to be a means of avoiding Internal Myopia. It offers the potential to enhance the benefits of STS and OSP approaches for even higher performance while avoiding their typical shortcomings. It builds systems thinking into daily roles and work activities. I call it the Outside-In approach because it comes at the design process from a different angle than past approaches.

It's called *Outside-In* because the design process starts outside the system to define its basic core tasks, focuses next on the interfaces and their tasks, and then moves inside to the task core process. It assumes no givens for the task core process until the *business core process* has been carefully studied and understood. The business core process consists of those tasks necessary for the survival and growth of the basic products or services rendered; it allows the parent organization to stay in business. The traditional approach, in contrast, is an *Inside-Out* approach. It begins with the task core process as its basis for design. It treats the parent system's definition of the task core process as a given.

This reversal in perspective and process can cause creative insights to emerge and lead the planners to innovative design configurations. For example, when looking from the outside in, the environmental scan is not something one does to understand the demands and pressures on the (predefined) task core process. It is something that is vital in order to understand accurately the broader business needs and to *define the basic core tasks* of the organization. Such subtle, but profound differences are characteristic throughout the process. What emerges is a true Open Systems Design that permits the organization to handle effectively the key interface tasks *continuously* as it also produces its outputs.

It's easier to appreciate the Outside-In framework when it's contrasted with the design models that have typically been used to date. A generic Inside-Out process could be described as follows:

1. Environmental scan to determine wants and needs of the core process.
2. Direction setting to specify output targets.
3. Core task analysis to clarify specific tasks to meet targets.
4. Definition of subsystem boundaries.
5. Design operating subsystems.
6. Design support subsystems.
7. Design managerial subsystems.
8. Design other subsystems (personnel, information, rewards, etc.).

This process has served many organizations well, especially when elements of Sociotechnical analysis and Open Systems Planning have been integrated into the various steps. Variations of it continue to cross my desk from time to time.[10] It has undoubtedly led to higher levels of performance than Machine Theory models. But, as previously noted, it has also developed its own set of unintended consequences. While focusing attention on improving the efficiency of the task core process, it also has played right into the hands of Internal Myopia. Frequently, so much energy is expended at the front end on the internal needs that there is little quality attention given to the interfaces — many of which are crucial for the system's overall business success. Enormous gains are possible in the first five to eight years, but then the effects of Internal Myopia set in to retard further development. In cases where the business environment shifts dramatically, the system finds itself no better than others in responding to changing needs. Table 4–3 contrasts Inside-Out and Outside-In approaches to demonstrate the differences more visibly.

The Dynamics of the Outside-In Approach

Let's leave the mechanics of Outside-In designing and investigate some of the dynamics of the process as it is used.

The organization embarking on such a process begins by seeking to understand what will be needed for overall business

Table 4–3

Comparison of Inside-Out and Outside-In Design Processes

Original Process (Inside-Out)	New Process (Outside-In)
1. **Environmental Scan:** Data gathering from the environment, company, and members of the system to determine wants, needs, and opportunities that the organization should meet. The focus is usually on wants, needs, and opportunities related to the defined *core process*. Environmental groups, related departments of the parent company, and members of the organization are usually surveyed.	1. **Environmental Scan:** The same as the original process, but the focus is on the *broader business issues* of the product or services offered. Cultural values and trends are examined in addition to wants, needs, and opportunities. Data are also gathered from a much broader range of company departments (not just direct interfaces) and competitors than those originally surveyed.
2. **Direction Setting:** Purpose, mission, objectives, and goals are established to provide clear direction for the organization's efforts. Again, the focus is primarily on the defined core process. Target areas typically include key results areas and employee development.	2. **Product Task Analysis:** Identification of the primary tasks of the system by scrutinizing the total products and services and answering the question, "Where can (and should) this organization make its contribution to exert maximum influence on the success of each product or service?"
3. **Core Task Analysis:** Identification of the core processes' primary tasks and the main activities involved in carrying out these tasks.	3. **Direction Setting:** Similar to the original process, but with broader focus on total business needs. Areas typically covered include contribution to products and services profitability and becoming partners in the business, as well as the core process.
4. **Define Subsystem Task Boundaries:** The various core tasks are subdivided into operating and support subsystems. All tasks deemed essential for producing the products and	4. **Define Organization Boundaries:** The specific product tasks that will be done entirely or in part by the organization are defined. Those tasks which are shared with other

Table 4–3

(Continued)

Original Process (Inside-Out)	New Process (Outside-In)
services are included in the operating subsystems. Tasks that provide for the support, maintenance, and strategic linkages of the system are included in the support subsystems.	organizations are examined and the definition of "who does what" is made.
5. **Design Operating Systems:** The tasks in the operating subunits are organized into roles. This defines what individuals will do in the system.	5. **Define Subsystem Task Boundaries:** The same as the original process.
6. **Design Support Systems:** The tasks in the support subunits are grouped into roles for individuals.	6. **Design Operating Systems:** The tasks in each of the operating systems are allocated to roles, beginning first with those tasks occurring at each subsystem's boundary. Once these interface tasks have been assigned, the operating core tasks are organized into roles.
7. **Design Managerial Systems:** The tasks related to leading and directing the core tasks in the subunits are grouped into managerial roles.	7. **Design Support Systems:** Same approach as above.
8. **Design Other Systems:** Systems of recruiting, training, information, and rewards are designed for the organization.	8. **Design Other Systems:** The same as the original process.
	9. **Overall Review:** Once the design sequence has been completed from the outside in, a review is made from the inside out to ensure compatibility, adjust for new learnings, and correct earlier assumptions which may be incorrect.

(continued)

Table 4–3
(Continued)

Original Process (Inside-Out)	New Process (Outside-In)

Key Differences

1. **Approach:** Focuses on the tasks at the core of the *transformation process* for the design emphasis. Once the core has been designed, the approach moves from inside to the outer parts of the system (support areas, managers, etc.). Hence, the designation of this approach as *inside out.*

1. **Approach:** Focuses on the tasks at the core of the *total product system* for the design emphasis. Many of these tasks are outside of an organization's traditional sphere of activity. The design approach gradually moves inward from the organization's interfaces to the core process. This is the outside-in approach. Also note the iterative step of rechecking the system from inside out as a review.

2. **Managerial Roles:** The inward focus of the design process leads to managerial roles that are largely *supervisory* in nature.

2. **Managerial Roles:** The outward focus leads to managerial roles which are more *flexible* in contributing to the *total* products and services needs.

3. **Employee Roles:** Emphasis on making the product as directed by management.

3. **Employee Roles:** Emphasis on managing and executing the daily core tasks to make the product or deliver the service. This is a prerequiste for managers if they are to assume their new roles.

4. **Effectiveness:** Effective in designing organizations to maximize the *core process.*

4. **Effectiveness:** Effective in maximizing the organization's *contribution to the products and services business needs.*

---

success. Based on this analysis, it then reviews all major tasks required for business success (see Figure 4–3 for an example) and asks the question, "Where can (and should) we contribute to exert maximum influence to the success of each product we make or each service we provide?" These initial steps are critical for remedying Internal Myopia. They wipe clean the predefined task list slate and build a new list based upon the overall business needs and the organization's unique abilities to contribute value-added effort. Some examples of what this looks like are found later in this chapter.

With this new set of tasks clearly in mind, the organization is in a position to develop purpose, mission, objectives, operating principles, and goals to codify the new direction. Dialogue with environmental interfaces then continues by specifying who does what when variations occur in task processes at the interface. This determines the actual operating boundary of the system and does much to resolve the interactions and expectations issues identified in traditional Open Systems Planning. It is this step that also ensures each subsystem in the parent organization does not head off in counterproductive or seriously overlapping directions.

The organization then subdivides the tasks into subsystems and begins designing each from the outside in. This is the point at which another key dynamic is introduced. Because interface tasks have been largely neglected in the past, they will no doubt become an addition to the managers' usual work load. How can they take on this new work load (deemed crucial to the overall success of the enterprise) and still do everything else? The answer is simple: They can't!

Now the other resources of the organization come under scrutiny to see how they might be utilized to take up the slack. So much for the "lid" that has been lodged atop developing STS/OSP work systems. Outside In thus creates a vacuum at the top to accomplish what the push from the bottom could not achieve: a lasting shift of responsibilities that will promote higher performance at all levels in the organization.

Outside-In designing produces higher levels of performance, with everyone winning in the process.

1. The organization wins because each subsystem takes on more responsibility to ensure overall business success. Because each system's added share is coordinated with others, the effort is synergistic rather than chaotic. Important activities no longer slip between the cracks of departmental roles. The overall effect of Outside In

is to increase productivity and operating efficiency against the priorities of the business core process.

2. Each subsystem wins because it is contributing in new and more meaningful ways that are closely tied to making a difference in the business results.

3. Managers win because they have assumed new roles on the leading edge of each subsystem's increased contribution. New perspective, new skills, and a new identity (a true partner in the business) make managerial roles more rewarding than ever.

4. Other employees win because they now have legitimized roles offering enormous personal growth and greater contribution to the business. Individuals capable of multiple skills and self-management are now a prerequisite for the rest of the dynamics.

Most importantly, the shift to higher performance is consistent, legitimized, and structured to be mutually reinforcing. When done properly, Outside-In designing can produce high performance rarely seen even in the best STS/OSP organizations to date.

It may be apparent from the foregoing description, but let's review exactly how Outside In addresses the six chronic signs of Internal Myopia.

1. The peaking-out syndrome exists only so long as lower levels of the organization begin growing and learning in a fixed set of parameters. These parameters are expanded considerably by Outside In; the tasks themselves are expanded to include more of the business core process and the roles of managers are altered to include a larger portion of boundary tasks as well as internal tasks. Responsibility for managing the daily operation (itself a highly variable situation) is given to capable individuals and work teams.

2. By now it should be clear that the Outside-In process breaks managers out of the traditional roles, or rigid management structure. The early stages of designing reorient managers to the enormous gain to be made if boundary management activities are undertaken as op-

posed to supervision only. Let me clarify at this point that I am not suggesting managers have nothing to do with the daily operation after going through the Outside-In process. The percentage of any manager's time allocated to boundary management and core work will vary from one situation to another, especially as a system matures over time. What I am suggesting is that in a reasonably mature operation, a large percentage of managerial time spent on boundary management will yield true high performance for the system. Under such conditions, managers must be discrete and sensitive when intervening in the core. All of this assumes that the needed development has taken place among their subordinates to handle greater responsibility.

3. Insecurity among first level managers has grown as a result of past incompatibilities between the traditional management structures and the innovative work systems developed in STS/OSP organizations. This incompatibility has left first level managers with the legitimate question, "What is my role now? What value can I add to the work process?" Their roles become clear, meaningful, and rewarding along with all others developed from the outside in.

An example of this comes from an experience I had working with some fifteen team managers in a STS/OSP manufacturing plant. Plant management wanted to develop work teams capable of greater autonomy in the daily work force. The plant leaders were concerned about how these team managers (many of whom had no college training but were good hands-on managers) would react to the team development program. We began working with each team manager from the outside in. After a few work sessions in which we had analyzed the environment of the work teams, the managers were surprised to learn all that could be done with their teams to optimize the business. Most of them had not even seen the opportunities in the environment because of their preoccupation with supervising their teams. In the months that followed, many of these managers successfully moved into new roles. Their teams took more responsibility for daily activities, the managers exerted greater influence in the system because of their boundary activities, and the plant became a high performer.

4. There has been friction between STS/OSP and environmental groups. Past methodologies have not spelled out collaborative interactions with the environment like Outside-In has. In order to specify "who does what" at the interfaces, there must be joint objectives and understanding for each other's role. Whether the environmental groups are suppliers, customers, or partners in a related function to the focal organization, they will have new appreciation and support for work designed from the outside in.

5. There has been inadequate flexibility in sharp business fluctuations. The number of organizations that have used Outside In is still relatively small. In those business sectors in which it has been used, the responsiveness has been greater than in other organizations. This is true even in the volatile computer industry, where Zilog and Digital Equipment have used Outside-In approaches to survive and even grow in the boom or bust dynamics of the 1980s. One should expect organizations designed from the outside in to be more effective at staying in touch with the relevant sectors of the environment. They should be more attuned to changes and have earlier warning signals that fluctuations are likely. Couple this awareness with the flexibility (in attitude and responsiveness) that comes from the Outside-In process, and it is not surprising that these systems will be better suited to combat the business environment. However, the current High Tech Age will continue to test our known limits of organizational performance.

6. There has been a blurry business rationale for design innovations. Innovative organizations that went through environmental tasks as exercises only were vulnerable to lose sight of business needs once their enthusiasm for the new system caught on. Outside In builds the perspective of the big picture into virtually every role. The

redefinition of organization tasks in the early stages usually avoids this problem.

In summary, Outside-In designing attacks Internal Myopia by creating a fundamental shift in how one views the organization's world. It causes one to view work from the perspective of a CEO in the beginning and then utilizes one's unique view from a specific sector to determine how higher performance levels could be achieved. Outside-In also systematically redesigns work roles at all levels to achieve high performance in a synergistic way. As we will now see in a couple of actual examples, the organizational energy released by this process is very great indeed.

Swanville: A Manufacturing Example of Outside In

The Swanville manufacturing plant was built in 1953 to manufacture rearview mirrors and related chrome trimmings for automobiles. The organizational planning for Swanville's inauguration was typical of the thinking of the day. The "assembly line mentality" permeated everything. Work was performed in a continuous flow and work stations were laid out along an assembly line. Employees were given clearly delineated tasks. Decisions usually followed the policy manual. There were four layers of management in the plant. Supervisors closely inspected the work of their subordinates. Under this regime, the plant enjoyed a rather prosperous history as the automobile industry boomed for the next two decades.

Starting with the oil crisis in the mid 1970s, however, top management in the corporate headquarters had become alarmed. The business cycle had definitely slowed down, and by 1984 there were some tough decisions on the table. One of them was whether or not to continue production at Swanville, or to consolidate all production into two newer facilities. Swanville's plant manager was informed of management's deliberation. The reason for Swanville's liability was obvious to all: its productivity and unit cost track records were simply out of line with other plants in the division.

The plant manager and his leadership team commissioned

an external organizational consultant and the plant Organization Development manager to lead them through a comprehensive redesign process. These consultants approached the situation from the outside in to see if Swanville could convince company management that it could compete in the 1980s and beyond. A small redesign team was formed to include:

- The plant manager.
- The operations managers: those who reported to the plant manager and headed up each operating and staff department in the plant. Together with the plant manager, they formed the plant's leadership team.
- Key department managers who managed the key work areas throughout the plant.

Let's recount the highlights that emerged from the outside in redesign process undertaken by this design team.

1. *Environmental scan* — The group drew a profile of the key environmental groups that would influence Swanville's survival (see Figure 4–2).

After carefully examining the trends, expectations, and interactions of each with the plant, the following themes emerged:

- The social environment would be characterized by increasing unemployment, employee mistrust, and increased employee demands for more information, more free time, and more responsibilities.
- The technical environment would see a myriad of new technologies coming such as robotics, automation, and computerization. This would lead to a change in the work people would do, the information available, and the skills required to do the work.
- Economically, the industry was likely to face stagnating markets, increased competition from foreign shores, and inflation of raw materials. It was felt that future investments would be much harder to justify.
- Company management was clearly saying that Swanville had to increase its productivity by 40 percent in three years and drastically improve its contribution to company profitability or face closing down. The keys to

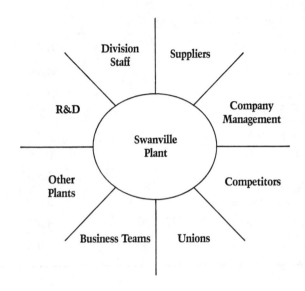

Figure 4–2
Environmental Scan for Swanville Plant

achieving this were focus on total unit costs versus the traditional manufacturing costs and becoming a partner in corporate profit improvement activities. Table 4–4 is a profit sheet for the mirrors produced at Swanville.

The Swanville leaders summarized the business needs facing the company and themselves.

- Increase overall flexibility of operation.
- Adapt to the changing economic situation.
- Decrease unit costs in order to increase the profit margin in spite of competition and inflation.
- Diversify plant activities (create more value-added to the company).

Table 4–4
Profit Sheet for Swanville Mirrors

Net Realization	100%
Product Cost	65.5%
Raw materials	33.5%
Packing materials	14.0%
Manufacturing expenses	10.0%
Delivery expenses	8.0%
Overheads	30.5%
Selling	6.5%
Market Research	2.5%
Research & Development	3.5%
Other (Corp. Admin.)	18.0%
Unit Profit	4.0%

In short, Swanville would have to continue controlling the manufacturing process while expanding its role beyond its present boundaries to create increased value-added.

2. *Product Task Analysis* — Now the group determined just exactly how the plant could increase its contribution in a significant way. It began by diagramming all the major tasks that were required to produce and deliver a mirror to the customer. A portion of the diagram looked like the product task analysis in Figure 4–3.

The planners asked themselves, "Where can we contribute in the improvement of the bottom-line profits of the company?" It was sobering to realize that even if the entire manufacturing expense were eliminated, it would still not be enough to match competition's profitability. Surely there had to be other ways to get back on track!

With the product tasks chart and the profit sheet in hand, the group finally settled on some possibilities for improved profitability. Figure 4–4 shows the product tasks diagram with the orig-

Consumer Research——Product Objectives——Product Specifications——Safety Testing

Process Definition——Equipment Design——Funding——Construction——Inspection——Construction Accounting

Product Test Planning——Special Product Tests——Master Plan Rollout

Supplier Qualification——Materials Ordering——Purchasing——Materials Delivery

Materials ——Mirror Production——Packaging——Product ——Shipments——Wholesalers'——Final Sale
Inspection   Storage   Handling

Employment Scheduling——Interviewing——Hiring——Plans Admin——Employee Relations——Training

Financial Analysis——Product Budget——Profit Forecasts——Cost Accounting——Plant Bookkeeping

Sourcing Rationalization——Plant Production Planning

Figure 4–3
Major Swanville Mirrors Tasks

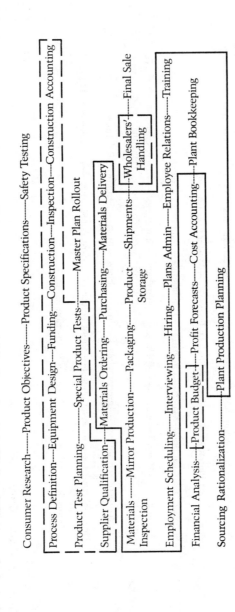

Figure 4–4
Swanville Task Analysis Depicting New Areas of Plant Involvement to Improve Corporate Business Results

inal plant tasks boxed in by the solid line and the new opportunities for plant contribution surrounded by dotted lines.

First, Swanville had to do some drastic redesigning of its own task core process to improve productivity.

Second, it could assume leadership for the company's total cost improvement by having a representative on the newly formed business team comprised of members from all corporate functions.

Third, it could take over certain engineering and personnel responsibilities currently handled at headquarters. The engineering tasks were closely related to the manufacturing process and were part of the corporate administration costs. Managers within the plant not only had the engineering skills, but also were more familiar with actual operating conditions and related equipment issues. The personnel tasks (recruiting, employee relations, training, and plans administration) were also things the plant felt it could do self-sufficiently in the future rather than relying on headquarters.

Fourth, it would seek to become the testing ground for new product forms. Such tests were usually disruptive to operating efficiencies and were usually a bone of contention between research and development and manufacturing. Yet, it was clear that considerable experimentation would be needed in the future if cheaper materials were to be used and new products released that would deliver improved performance at a lower cost. Currently, there was no plant that handled experiments reliably, causing many tests to be rerun several times.

Fifth, the company was clearly studying the possibilities of using new metal alloys and synthetic materials that would uphold the product image, perform as well or better, and drastically reduce costs. New suppliers and raw materials would need to be cultivated and tested. Swanville wanted this business.

3. *Direction setting* — The group defined its mission as follows: "We will ensure our continuity by becoming the best and lowest cost producer within our shipping zone. We will fight to attract additional production from new product lines. We will become a development center for corporate innovations."

This would represent a truly unique contribution to the company, if fulfilled. From this mission flowed the following objectives:

- Aggressively improve plant productivity by 15 percent per year for the next three years.
- Enhance productivity through new technologies such as computerization, robotics, and automation.
- Build an organization in which all employees will have willingness, tools, and skills to ensure achievement of the plant mission.
- Be a contributing partner in activities and decisions related to business development.

Other documents were produced to clarify the direction the plant would need to be pursuing. Operating principles were defined that spelled a new culture for the plant. This would be one in which people:

- Work in teams.
- Strive for excellence in all they do.
- Achieve personal development through the accomplishment of work.
- Respond to whatever the business requires.
- Know how the company is faring in the competitive world and how their personal effort contributes to success or failure.
- Have all necessary information to do their work.
- Decide matters where they have the most knowledge and expertise.

This was a cultural shift of no small proportions! The leadership was convinced such a shift was the only hope to improve productivity by the targeted amounts. The plant strategy served management well when discussing the business needs for changing the way the plant did its work. Numerous discussions were held with employees in all departments. In time both union officials and employees were convinced that major change was the only way to save the plant. They gave their support to the effort.

4. *Organization boundary definition* — Now discussions were initiated with the various interface groups to determine precisely the definition of organizational boundaries. Conversations with the division manager and manufacturing director led to

agreements for a plant representative to be a member of the business team. Such representation would not come "free," however. The business team would require manufacturing support for many new initiatives, some of which would take years before improving things on the shop floor. The engineering department agreed to changes that would move a large portion of what it did into the plant organization. Personnel also agreed to some shifts of responsibility, providing that the plant personnel department participated in policy formulation on matters affecting the entire company. R&D was an intrigued (though skeptical) recipient of Swanville's proposal to become the testing ground for new products and materials. Several lengthy discussions finally determined how R&D and the plant would collaborate on future tests. The buying department agreed to work with Swanville managers and new suppliers to initiate qualification and testing procedures.

This entire process took months to complete, but was critical in developing a clear understanding for what Swanville was going to undertake. The design team met periodically during this period to review progress, define further principles, set new targets, assign follow-up activities, and check the pulse of the change effort. Company management was supportive of the plant's new mission and strategic direction. This support was instrumental in getting the central staff groups to agree to the shifts in responsibility. Key outside groups were now clear on how they would work with the plant in the future. Most importantly, the plant and its employees now knew precisely how they could contribute to improved corporate results.

5. *Subsystem task boundary definition* — Swanville's organization looked like Figure 4–5 at the beginning of the design process. Each operating and staff group had its own organization headed by an operations manager, who was a member of the plant leadership team.

Using the Sociotechnical criteria, the group found that some of the departmental lines did not promote effective work. For instance, the central machine shop contained vital resources that were needed spontaneously on the production lines. Efficiency suffered every time a mechanic had to be called for. Likewise, the quality lab had been organized separately from the production area, even though quality inspections occurred on the

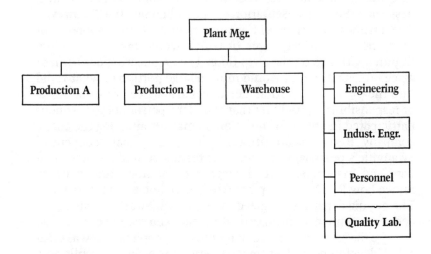

Figure 4–5
Swanville Plant Organization at the Beginning of Outside-In Design Work

lines. The staff groups collectively represented a fairly large overhead that appeared to be larger than needed.

Based on a more critical evaluation of the work flow, the natural breaks in the process proved to be warehousing, production, engineering, and plant support. Thus the new plant structure was designed to support these natural units. The new structure looked like Figure 4–6.

6. *Operating systems design* — The operating system design, or production module, had to be organized to handle a greater number of tasks. In addition to the production tasks it had traditionally executed, the production module now was responsible for its own maintenance, quality control, scheduling, cost savings projects, and personnel management. All of these tasks had previously been handled by staff groups. Additionally, the module now shouldered many of the new responsibilities from outside, such as manufacturing representation on the business team, engineering of small projects, new supplier development, and new

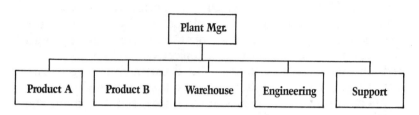

Figure 4–6
Swanville Plant Organization as a Result of Outside-In Design Work

product tests. Following the outside-in approach, these interface tasks were the first to be examined.

The operations manager, as head of the module, was the likely choice to represent the plant on the business team. This would prove to be a role that would require 30 percent to 50 percent of this person's time to be spent away from the module's daily business. The engineering tasks, new supplier development, and new product tests were assigned to an experienced department manager who would head up the functions of maintenance, quality, and cost control. The other new functions (normal maintenance, scheduling, and personnel management) were assigned to the department manager over production.

The additional work load caused the managerial roles at all levels to shift dramatically. Here is a summary of the generic responsibilities for each level:

The *operations manager's primary role* consisted of three main priorities: (1) serving as the module's link to the rest of the company as the manufacturing representative on the business team, (2) ensuring that medium- to long-term objectives were clear in the module and that continual progress was being made toward them, and (3) ensuring that all individuals in the module were developing skills and contributing in greater ways over time.

The *department managers* divided up the additional tasks that had been imported from the outside. These included the engineering of small projects, new supplier development, new product tests, daily maintenance, quality control, scheduling, cost savings projects, and personnel management. As agreed with the operations manager, these department managers interacted with other company functions to ensure objectives in these areas were met and standards were upheld. The department manager team was also responsible for short-term results, operational improvements to ensure better results in the future, and developing the first level managers and production teams.

The *first level managers* each shared in some of the projects being coordinated by the department manager team. Each was also responsible for the results of a specific operation area, including production, cost, quality, maintenance, and personnel. First level managers coached the production teams by reviewing business needs with them, helping them to meet those needs, providing feedback on results and ways to improve, and helping the team to assume more responsibility over time.

The *production teams* set short-term goals consistent with the business needs, made operating decisions, and initiated problem solving around the basic core tasks of the module: production, maintenance, quality, and cost control. The teams usually had one or more team members who coordinated the major work areas.

It should be noted that every level in the production module had a combination of boundary and interface tasks and internal core tasks. This shift in roles required some time for all to adapt, but was eagerly received because it provided meaningful growth to all and was clearly the means for increasing the plant's contribution to business results.

7. *Support systems design* — The outside-in process was also used in the support group and the engineering group design. These were both very small modules, but provided needed linkage between the production modules and the corporate headquarters. They also provided valuable training to managers and production team members who were taking over tasks in these areas.

8. *Designing other crucial systems* — The Swanville design group now examined the other support systems in the plant to see what modifications would be necessary to reinforce the

changes in the way the plant operated. They found changes were required in all of the following:

- *Personnel.* Recruiting and selection procedures would have to be revised to match a more demanding profile in the future. The quality of good teamwork and self-management were added to the technical qualifications that had been used in the past. Training would be required to help all levels become proficient in their new roles.
- *Rewards systems.* Pay and rewards systems would have to be revised to fit the boundary and internal balance at all levels. The hourly wage system was changed to reinforce the value of developing multiskills and self-management.
- *Decision making and control systems.* A few policy changes were required to align policies with the new role requirements for decision making (i.e., the operations manager no longer needed to approve parts to be used in equipment repairs; the department manager was authorized).
- *Information systems.* There was a general loosening up of reports and information to the lower levels of the organization. For example, relevant data on company developments no longer stayed on the plant manager's desk. The assigned department manager and first level managers also received it. Production teams now got their daily reports directly. Monthly summaries of all key factors also went directly to the teams.

All of these changes were made gradually over the ensuing eighteen months. This time was required to accomplish the training, redeployment of certain individuals on teams to ensure balance, and identification of specific projects. But, because the design end points were clear, attrition was used as a natural ally for the productivity improvements. Hiring was suspended until the plant's enrollment was adequate to meet the new design specifications and ensure a lasting productivity improvement. The productivity improvement in staffing alone was approximately 10 percent of 325 employees. The operating efficiencies, however, rose to the point that total productivity remained on track at 15 percent per year. Major cost improvements were conceived and delivered by the business team. The other boundary tasks assumed by Swanville also began to pay off. As of this writing, the plant's performance has improved dramatically — in line with the promises it made to company management. Although the industry is still tight and the future uncertain, Swanville is very much alive and kicking!

Fleming: A Purchasing Office Example of Outside In

The Fleming Company is a toilet goods firm on the West Coast. Because of a companywide effort to improve its efficiencies and market orientation, the purchasing office had been coming under heavy scrutiny. The general manager was not satisfied with the buyers' ability to respond to market needs, and the group was in the midst of making improvements to be more efficient in its core work. The head of the purchasing department commissioned a small diagonal slice of the office (managers, clerks, and secretaries) to work with an organizational consultant to examine the situation from the outside in and recommended what further improvements to make.

Understanding the Business Situation

The group began by scanning its environment to better understand the business needs and competitive realities facing the company. Figure 4–7 shows the major groups that interacted with the purchasing office. The design team learned from this process that the work it had done to streamline the corporate purchasing process was appreciated and paying off for the company. However, its customer service needed to improve. The company's responsiveness to changes in the market was still not acceptable and the purchasing function could play a key role in future improvements.

Next, they analyzed all the tasks needed to put the company's products on the store shelf. This analysis yielded some im-

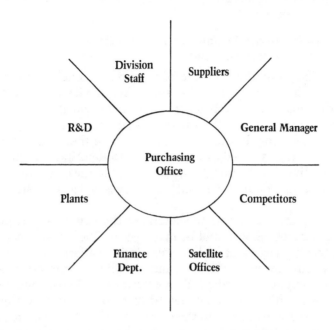

Figure 4–7
Fleming Environmental Scan

portant new insights. As the group mapped out what it currently did, virtually everything was centered on keeping the pipeline full of raw materials to be converted into finished product. No one doubted the necessity of this core process. However, the group itself saw that little was being done to use their information to forge strategic advantages for the company.

For instance, as ingredient prices fluctuated, one could save (or lose) an enormous amount of money (a 1 percent cost variation in all materials was equal to $1 million!). Inventories could be reduced if purchasing ordered raw materials to arrive at the plant just in time for production. A 5 percent improvement in this area would avoid $1 million in expenditures and save $100 million annually in inventory capital costs. However, at present no one was doing anything that would allow this kind of synchronization to occur.

Defining the Business Strategy to Fit the Business Situation

The group then considered what purchasing's purpose and mission should be. There were some diverse viewpoints at first, but the group soon reached consensus and decided that responding to the demands of their major clients (general management, plants, operating divisions, R&D) was to be their major thrust. Moreover, they wanted to be partners with R&D and manufacturing to deliver breakthrough capital savings to the company. Based on this sense of purpose, specific objectives and goals were established.

The next step was to sketch out the new tasks the group thought purchasing should be involved in. These tasks included strategic management of key areas (price variations, inventory levels, alternative materials, and suppliers), marketing team membership, close divisional interactions, and cost savings initiatives. In this case, there was little need to negotiate this expanded role with others in the company. They had been requesting such involvement, but purchasing had been too busy with its prime task of keeping the pipeline full. The organization design problem now facing the group was how to take on this additional work without sacrificing efficiency in the pipeline core process.

Fitting Design to the Strategy

The process then moved to examining the natural breaks in the purchasing process. As opposed to an organization structure that had broken the department into eight materials desks and one central typing pool, this process analysis indicated there were really three major categories of raw materials that could be managed relatively independently of each other. Within these categories the need for teamwork was very high.

Each of these category groups was renamed a *performance center* and was designed from the outside in. Each performance center was staffed by a team of buyers, assistant buyers, and clerical support. Because they were all familiar with the dynamics of their raw materials, they could assist each other better than be-

Core Areas Coordination
Marketing Team Member
Divisional Representative
Cost Savings Project Leader

↓

Buyer

↓

Purchasing Logistics
Suppliers – Plants Interface

↓

Assistant Buyers

↓

Clerical Work
Information & Document Requests

↓

Clerical Support

↓

Automation

Figure 4–8
Fleming Task Reallocation Across Organizational Levels Based on Outside-In Design Work

fore. Figure 4–8 shows how the tasks were distributed following the outside-in process.

As in the situation with Swanville, Fleming's purchasing office found the outside-in process to allow everyone to win. Each level in the organization assumed additional tasks to give them a combination of boundary and internal core tasks. The capacity for this additional load stemmed from two sources: they restructured themselves into teams to allow more cooperation and teamwork and automated many of the information processing functions that had been done manually. Each performance center was authorized to purchase computers and other automation devices to improve the efficiency of recording data, creating documents, and telecommunications. Additional work was done in the following months to provide training for the new roles and clarify the new information needs of each individual. The changes in roles at each level were discussed thoroughly with those affected, especially other company groups (research and development, the plants, and general management). Agreements were reached on Fleming's new task boundaries. As the project was initiated, two immediate benefits were realized. One was the elimination of all overtime. The other was a freeing up of 15 percent of the departmental resources' time to pursue the new activities. Thus, the group began pursuing additional work on key business core tasks with a major productivity improvement!

Conclusion

This chapter has described the process of designing a complex organization to achieve high performance. I have outlined one of the major flaws up to now in organization designing — the failure to attack the symptoms of Internal Myopia. Attention to the internal task core process is certainly needed, but must be managed skillfully for the system not to become oblivious to the environment. The Outside-In design approach has been described here as a means of addressing Internal Myopia. In the situations in which this approach has been used, it has been effective in creating a healthy balance between boundary interface tasks and internal tasks.

Designing organizations is an exhaustive undertaking when done properly. It requires a thoughtful assessment of the business situation facing the organization and the work requirements needed to meet the environmental demands. It also requires painstaking work to fashion the organization design elements so that they fit with each other and reinforce high performance. But the rewards are greater than the effort spent. High performance, channeled in the directions you want, can be the result of such a process.

Notes

1. J. R. Galbraith, *Organization design* (Reading, Mass.: Addison-Wesley, 1977); J. R. Galbraith and D. A. Nathanson, *Strategy implementation: The role of structure and process* (St. Paul, Minn.: West, 1978); I. C. MacMillan and P. E. Jones, "Designing organizations to compete," *The Journal of Business Strategy* (Spring 1984):11–26; P. B. Vail, "The purposing of high-performing systems," *Organizational Dynamics* (Autumn 1982):23–39.

2. E. L. Trist and K. W. Bamforth, "Some social and psychological consequences of the long-wall method of coal-getting," *Human Relations* 4:3–38; W. A. Pasmore and J. J. Sherwood, eds., *Sociotechnical systems: A sourcebook* (La Jolla, Calif.: University Associates, 1978).

3. F. E. Emery and E. L. Trist, "Socio-technical systems," in C. W. Churchman and M. Verhuist, eds., *Management sciences models and techniques*, Vol. 2 (London: Pergamon Press, 1960), 83–97.

4. Ibid.

5. P. Hill, *Towards a new philosophy of management* (Epping, Essex, Great Britain: Gower Press, 1976); W. A. Pasmore and J. J. Sherwood, eds., *Sociotechnical systems: A sourcebook* (La Jolla, Calif.: University Associates, 1978), 225–312; C. Pava, *Managing new office technology — An organizational strategy* (New York: Free Press, 1983).

6. A. B. Cherns, "The principles of sociotechnical design," *Human Relations*, 29 (1976): 783–792.

7. G. K. Jayaram, "Open systems planning," in W. G. Bennis, K. D. Benne, R. Chin, and K. E. Corey, eds., *The Planning Of Change*, 3rd ed. (New York: Holt, Rinehart and Winston, 1976).

8. O. Elliott, "Beyond sociotechnical/open system design " (Paper presented at the forty-fifth National Academy of Management Conference, Boston, Mass., 1984); O. Elliott, A. B. Shani, and D. P. Hanna, "Strategic thinking and sociotechnical system design: A high tech merger" (Paper presented at the twenty-sixth Annual Conference of the Western Academy of Management, San Diego, Calif., 1985).

9. R. E. Walton and L. S. Schlesinger, "Do supervisors thrive in participative work systems?" *Organizational Dynamics* (Winter 1979):24–38.

10. Charles Krone, "Open systems redesign," in W. W. Burke, ed., *New technologies in organization development: II* (La Jolla, Calif.: University Associates, 1974); D. A. Nadler and M. L. Tushman, *Concepts for the design of organizations* (OR&C Inc, 1982); H. E. Stokes, "Organizational effectiveness planning — a process for organization renewal and revitalization," unpublished paper, 1986; W. Veltrop, "Designing for high performance in a changing environment," unpublished paper, 1986.

5

Approaches to Specific Design Issues

The Outside-In approach is a general framework for designing High Performance Organizations. It provides a road map for design, but requires supporting guidelines for making the many design decisions that will lead to high performance. This chapter explores some guidelines that may be used for making specific design decisions in three crucial areas:

- Determining departmental boundaries.
- Organizing work teams.
- Structuring individual work roles.

Let's begin by reviewing characteristics of living (open) systems and principles that many high performers have found useful in optimizing these characteristics. This will describe an ideal standard that one would hope to achieve at each of these three levels of organization.

Principles for Organizing Living Systems

There are a few key principles that seem to be common to most of the high performers I have been exposed to in several different companies and industries. Each principle makes its own unique contribution to exposing characteristics inherent in living systems. The primary characteristics of living systems are:

- They are purposeful and goal directed.
- They are self-regulating (core processes) to achieve their purpose.
- They require goal clarity, goal commitment, clear feedback, and reasonable autonomy in order to be self-regulating.
- Those who survive are able to adapt successfully to environmental changes. This requires maintaining an acceptable steady state and at the same time being able to change their purpose when required by a major environmental shift.

The challenge, then, for the organization designer is to create self-regulating (or self-sufficient) work units that are capable of high performance amidst changing environmental circumstances. Many high performers have based their approaches on principles derived from Sociotechnical Systems theory and from research like that done by Dr. J. Richard Hackman of the Harvard Business School.[1]

You will recall that Sociotechnical theory articulated some key principles that were recommended for developing self-sufficient work units:

- Control variances as close as possible to their point of origin.
- Develop multiskills in each member of the system.
- Provide information to the point of action and problem solving.

Based on further work done by Sociotechnical consultants and complementary efforts by Dr. Hackman, I summarize the key principles for effectively organizing living systems as follows:

1. *Skill variety.* The work should require a variety of different activities involving the use of several different skills and talents. For example, rather than endlessly

tightening bolts on an automobile assembly line, the individual might also control inventory, make quality inspections, train new employees, and conduct qualification testing for new parts.

2. *Task identity.* The job should be to complete a whole and identifiable piece of work, that is, doing the job from beginning to end with a visible outcome. Preparatory and auxiliary tasks are often included in a single role to create this sense of the whole task. For example, one engineer might be responsible for making a project recommendation, developing the project budget, executing the project in line with budget and objectives, and evaluating the final quality of the work.

3. *Task significance.* The work done should have a substantial impact on the lives of other people, whether those people are in the immediate organization or in society at large. The work should also make some perceivable contribution to the end product of the unit. For example, collecting samples for product testing might rate low in this area; conducting the product test itself and reporting the results might rate high.

4. *Feedback.* The work itself should provide individuals with direct and clear information about the effectiveness of their performance. For example, production efficiency reports, actual monies spent versus the budgeted amount, amount of overtime, and the number of insurance claims reprocessed due to clerical errors are all examples of feedback that is generated by the performance of the individual or work unit.

5. *Autonomy.* The work should provide freedom, independence, and discretion to the individual in scheduling the work and in determining the procedures to be used in carrying it out. For example, production team members determine when to shut down for repairs, divide operating tasks among themselves on a daily basis, and determine their annual vacation schedule.

6. *Teamwork.* Individual roles should be grouped into small work teams when any or all of the following conditions exist:

- There is a necessary interdependence between individual roles.
- There is a relatively high level of stress in the individual tasks.
- The individual jobs do not make an obvious, perceivable contribution to the end product.

When such conditions exist, team effectiveness is enhanced when team members have interlocking tasks, rotate jobs at some frequency, and work in physical proximity to one another. For example, a small work group might be charged with cleaning and maintaining the total building rather than assigning individuals to sweep only floors or clean just specific areas.

Although specific applications may vary from organization to organization, most high performers have based their work design upon these or similar principles. It is interesting to note that managerial roles are usually more congruent with these principles than other roles. Tradition has taught us to solve motivation problems at the lowest levels of the organization with "carrot and stick" incentives, closer supervision, and more penetration by management. The high performers have found the approach that delivers a lasting improvement is the one that begins by redesigning work at the lower levels of the organization to be more like work done at the top! Intrinsic motivation, ownership, and self-regulation are the typical results when this redesign is done well.

As you are about to see, another fundamental shift stimulated by the research on work design causes us to view work as a process (comprised of task, individual, and group elements) rather than as a series of unrelated steps. Keeping in mind the principles discussed in this section, let's now look at some examples of applying them at the departmental, team, and individual levels.

Determining Departmental Boundaries

One step of the Outside-In approach called for determining subsystem or departmental boundaries. We are indebted to the Sociotechnical theorists for providing a sound, analytical approach to this difficult task. The Sociotechnical method begins by laying out the work process to be organized. This process is a series of tasks that follow the input — transformation — output sequence outlined in Open Systems Theory. For instance, the following task flow might be typical in a printing shop:

Job delivered by customer → Work order form completed → Due date finalized → Job assigned to be completed→Page layouts done→Printing completed→Job checked for errors→Job sorted/collated→Customer notified→Job picked up by customer

The next step is to identify where the natural breaks in the process occur. These breaks provide clues for identifying the self-sufficient subsystems. The Sociotechnical term for each subsystem is *unit operation*. The unit operation's boundary is formed by a *state change in the input*. Such a state change may refer to an actual change in the raw material's form or a change of location or storage of the material. Attention is placed on the series of transformations through which the raw material goes rather than the operations of control, checking, verification, or inspection. This is an important concept because there are usually fewer divisions based on changes to the input than divisions based on checking and control. Put another way, departments created by the Sociotechnical process will be relatively larger and more naturally self-sufficient than those created by conventional wisdom.

How would you departmentalize the process flow of our printing shop? Try your hand at determining where the process should be divided to efficiently handle large work loads. The printing shop had actually divided this process into five subsystems (two departments — scheduling and printing) with one or more employees to handle each.

1. A receiving clerk accepted the customer's job and completed the work order form.
2. Supervisor A checked the legibility of the work order form, finalized the due date in light of other work order priorities, and assigned the job to be completed.
3. Ten printers processed the work assignments by laying out the pages as specified and printing the number of copies ordered.

4. Supervisor B checked the finished jobs for errors. When errors were found, the job was returned to the printer for correction. Those without errors were passed on to the assembly clerk.

5. The assembly clerk assembled and collated the job as necessary and notified the customer, who picked it up.

Now, how many unit operations are there in this process based on a Sociotechnical analysis of state changes to the inputs? There are only *three* transformations that the customer's order undergoes in the printing process:

1. From order to page layout.
2. From page layout to printed copy.
3. From printed copy to assembled and collated sets.

With that as our guideline, we can examine this process more closely to determine how the current five subdivisions might be changed to create more self-sufficient work units. I have used this example in several training situations and found that, when following the work design guidelines outlined here, most solutions are characterized by one department with fewer total employees and two to three subdivisions in the process. Many managers also create small customer-aligned teams that handle the entire process while periodically rotating assignments between the unit operations.

Identifying the unit operations alone doesn't always settle the issue of where to place departmental boundaries. Depending on the sheer volume and complexity of work to be processed, there are some other factors that may have to be considered. The most common factors are technology, territory, and time.[2] Each should be considered to determine if they impose limitations on the ability of the individual or work team to be self-sufficient in completing the work process.

Technology, for example, may be so complex and differentiated that no single individual or work group could competently handle all of the unit operations. If this were true, then departmentalization might be required for different units of operation. This is not the case in our printing shop, for instance, where the different unit operations are closely related technically or are simple manual operations. In fact, each of the three unit operations could be done by the same person. But if the process were that of making toilet paper, the situation would be very different. Papermaking technology itself is a complex science as is converting the paper into the desired final product. The complexity of these two unit operations might require different departments to competently handle them.

Territory is another factor to consider. If equipment or other realities make physical proximity throughout the entire process an impossibility, then geographical departmentalization might be required to maintain the needed focus and support. An example of this is a sales force divided into geographical districts. The work process is essentially the same, but the territorial demands of the entire country exceed what one district could adequately handle.

Time requires differentiation when the task exceeds the allotted schedule for an individual or work group to complete the process. Continuous production processes that run around the clock are an example of this factor. Work shifts divide the task into manageable bits to be handled. Another dimension of the time factor is the relative time orientation (long-term, short-term) called for by the work itself. For example, a pure research function might be miscast if included in a project group. The long-term orientation of the researchers would be at odds with the "get it done now" mentality of the project group and vice versa. Both might be distracted by an incompatible time perspective when it became necessary to set goals, define priorities, or agree on deadlines. If there is a great difference in the time orientation of different tasks, it may be advisable to separate them.

There are two other factors that might also need evaluation to determine if they would negatively affect the self-sufficiency of the work unit:

- *Interdependence with other departmental resources.* If the work unit must constantly reach across an organizational boundary for needed resources to complete the process, then it is not self-sufficient. Attention should be given to locating the needed resources inside the department where they are used on a regular basis. This can be done through job rotation, cross-training, or structural reallocation of resources.

- *Group size.* Self-sufficiency is hard to develop if the work group is too large. Optimal group size ranges from three to fourteen members. Groups larger than this will find it more difficult to make decisions, maintain physical proximity, and share the work effectively.

No organization will be able to optimize itself in all of these boundary issues. Each boundary choice represents a trade-off, determining which organizational characteristics to reinforce and which problems to live with. Ideally, the design would seek the optimum fit among all these factors. Having considered where to place departmental boundaries from these different perspectives, however, the odds are much greater that the departments will be inherently capable of self-regulation and high performance. One key perception shift that occurs in such work designs is that individuals relate more with the end result than with anything else. Operators, tradespersons, clerks, and supervisors all think of themselves as "making toilet paper" or "providing the best legal counsel" or "selling homes."

One sterling example of these principles in action is a manufacturing plant in Pine Valley. The Pine Valley plant manufactures three different aerosol spray products. Small work crews are responsible for the entire work process for each product — from receipt of raw materials to shipping at the warehouse dock. All related tasks — production, quality control, cleanup, scheduling, and equipment modifications are handled by a team of sixteen to twenty-four people. Each team rotates across three shifts without a direct shift supervisor. The entire plant is sliced into three departments, each supported by a few small staff groups. Pine Valley's record for efficiency, reliability, and low-cost production are unequalled in its industry.

Contrast this with a typical government agency in West Germany organized to issue automobile license plates. The work process is relatively simple:

1. Record personal data of the automobile owner(s).
2. Assign license plate number.
3. Issue license plate.
4. Collect license fee.

Each step in the process is handled by a different civil servant and the applicants are required to go to a different building to have the license plate made (while they wait!) before returning to the original building to pay the fee. Each person does his or her assigned job with precision in a process that can last several hours if the lines are long or an unusual case is being handled. I have never seen a clearer example of a process that was simultaneously in control and inefficient!

In summary, these guidelines are aimed at creating self-sufficient work units in which the individuals identify more with the product or service delivered than with anything else. These principles break up the monolithic bureaucracies into modern versions of the family business: small, lean work groups focused on a significant output that is valued by the local community. The experience to date is that such work groups are largely self-regulating and therefore require less supervision than traditionally applied in the past. But most importantly, they are divided according to natural boundaries (related to the work flow) rather than artificial divisions to maintain ease of control and supervision.

Organizing Work Teams

If the process analysis has been done thoroughly to determine the departmental boundaries, then much of the work to design effective team structures will already have been done. Teams are merely work units formed to complete a set of interdependent tasks that cannot be handled by a single individual. The unit operations analysis is extremely valuable in identifying where the interdependencies do and do not exist. Figure 5–1 represents a team design checklist that is based on the principles explained earlier. Let's apply this checklist to a couple of work teams to see if they are designed for high performance.

A team called the Packers worked in a factory making upholstery for furniture makers. The team was comprised of nine individuals. They worked on an assembly line that was thirty yards long. Two Packers were responsible for checking raw material quality and loading the different fabrics onto the looms. Four operators were responsible for adjusting the equipment to keep

Team Design Checklist

1. *Will it be a real team?*

   _____ Will the members be truly interdependent? Will they have to cooperate in order to complete their tasks?

   _____ Will each member's role be differentiated from others so it makes a unique contribution to the result?

   _____ Will there be enough physical proximity for team identity to be easily observable?

2. *Will it be a work team?*

   _____ Will the team have a whole task (inputs—transformations—outputs) so that a product or service is produced?

3. *Will the right resources be on the team?*

   _____ Will team members have the necessary knowledge and skills to complete the whole task?

   _____ Will the team have enough people to do the task—but no more than necessary?

4. *Will it be a self-sufficient team?*

   _____ Will the team have authority to determine who does what by when for daily activities?

   _____ Will the team get accurate and timely information about its results, operating standards, and new developments that will affect daily priorities?

   _____ Will leadership be shared among team members so that no one person is the "straw boss?"

Figure 5–1
Checklist for Designing an Effective Work Team

the weaving process under control. Process variations occurred frequently and required that many adjustments be made "on the run." One team member checked the quality of the product at regular intervals and recorded the inspection results on a form that was stored for future reference. Two team members worked in the packing area, where equipment rolled the fabric and cut it so they could bundle it for shipping. They packed the bundles into large crates and sent them to the dock for further transport.

Each member of the Packers rotated to different assignments from time to time. Having worked together for over six years, everyone now was able to handle any task on the assembly line. Their ability to move along the assembly line, helping each other as needed, was impressive. The operation ran twenty-four hours a day, seven days a week. Team members relieved each other for lunch and break periods. They shared housekeeping responsibilities for their area. The equipment was shut down for one day every three months for maintenance and repair, which the Packers did much of with the assistance of technical specialists from the maintenance department.

Each work shift began with a thirty-minute team meeting in which team members shared coordinating responsibility for planning, problem solving, and evaluating some aspect of the Packers' performance. Production efficiencies, quality results, cost improvements, training, maintenance lists, team effectiveness, safety, housekeeping, and administration were each coordinated by a different team member. The production coordinator was officially recognized as the team leader and "tie breaker" if the decision-making process got hung up, but such instances were quite rare. Three team members had served as production coordinator in the past six years. All coordinator positions were rotated just like the operating assignments were. The team reported to a department manager, who was responsible for results on the Packers' line across all three shifts. The Packers had operated without a shift supervisor for over six years. When this latter change was made, all mail that used to go to the shift supervisor began going directly to the team.

The Packers were the talk of the factory. Their business results were the best in the entire company and their work standards were equal or superior to any other team. Employees from other teams, who occasionally filled in for absentees, often said they would give anything to be able to stay on permanently.

This actual example of high performance should come as no surprise to you. As you can see from the team design checklist, the Packers were perfectly designed to get these impressive results.

Now, let's consider another team, the Freeloaders. The Freeloaders were a warehouse crew in a case goods factory. They were comprised of forty hard-working team members who had responsibility for storing incoming raw materials, monitoring inventories, and shipping finished product cases to wholesalers. The raw materials tasks consisted of unloading trucks and rail cars (using forklift trucks) and stacking raw materials in the warehouse until the production area needed them. Some materials had to be sorted and prepared by the Freeloaders before they could be used in production. Quality defects or short counts were logged by the Freeloaders and sent to the supplier for credit. The finished product tasks were centered on a conveyor system that brought products from the production area to a unit load former. The unit load former arranged the cases in a stacked unit and wrapped them in a plastic film in preparation for shipping. These units were then shipped by truck or rail. Depending on the schedule, units went from the load former to a storage space in the warehouse or directly to the dock. Sophisticated inventory procedures were used to accurately locate the product and ensure that first in — first out rotation occurred.

The forty-member Freeloader team was responsible for the entire warehouse procedure. Daily team meetings gave the Freeloaders' shift supervisor the opportunity to finalize each person's assignment for the shift and to share information (results from the previous day, new developments, company news, etc.). Typically, the team members were found in four main clusters during the shift: the truck dock (loading and unloading), the rail (loading and unloading), the unit load former (loading units and storing in the warehouse), and the raw materials area (inspecting quality and assessing damages). Naturally, some team members in these areas were constantly on the move, picking up or delivering cases.

Like the Packers, the Freeloaders had some coordination and administrative responsibilities to enrich their task variety. There were coordinators for safety, cost control, truck maintenance, training, housekeeping, team effectiveness, and administration. These responsibilities were handled by three to five team members, who worked under direction of the shift supervisor.

The Freeloaders were a competent team — their results were slightly above the company average. Despite this, they seemed to have continual personnel problems. Team decision making was a difficult process. Management decisions were frequently second-guessed. Team morale was not very high, though each individual did a capable job.

Now, how do the Freeloaders match up to the team design checklist?

Obviously, the Freeloaders meet many of the criteria of the checklist and they are a functioning team. But is the team a high performer? In my opnion it is not. The checklist can help us pinpoint some areas to redesign so that this team could become a high performer.

- Physical proximity is a problem for the Freeloaders. Although they are organized to complete the whole task, this task is spread over a territory of thirty acres under one roof! It might be warranted to examine the unit operations for the Freeloaders' task to see if some subdivisions might make teamwork more meaningful. In fact, the unit operations reveal four potential subdivisions: the truck dock, the rail, the unit load former, and the raw materials area.
- The Freeloaders have enough people to do the task, but far more than is practical for an effective team operation. Forty people is more like a mob than a team. Subdividing the task into smaller teams would certainly alleviate this problem.
- The Freeloaders are self-sufficient in the physical tasks, but are not in the coordination and administrative areas. As the work shift rolls out each day, each Freeloader goes about the assigned task with relative autonomy. But they have little autonomy in meaningful decision making or similar coordination functions.

We see in this case that design decisions frequently can select only the lesser of two evils. In the desire to preserve integrity of the whole task (the warehousing process), the designers of the Freeloaders crew have created some other problems. Address these problems and you run the risk of compartmentalizing work into less meaningful units. This is the point at which the unit operations analysis can be so invaluable! In reality, the warehousing process does have some smaller whole tasks, defined as unit operations. In this case, the designer could create smaller work teams built around the unit operations (dock, rail, load former, raw materials). Identification with the total end result could be achieved through job rotation, where, like the Packers, crew members worked in each of the unit operations over time. Another option, one exercised by Pine Valley, is to combine the warehousing function with production and create one team that handles the true whole task from start to finish. The specific technologies and space requirements will determine how viable this option would be for the Freeloaders.

Obviously, such decisions in real life require careful scrutiny and weighing of the pros and cons of each issue. What I hope is clear through these examples is that the design principles reviewed here can be useful in making organization design decisions based on principle, not by default!

Structuring Individual Work Roles

The literature is full of experiences focused on enlarging and enriching individual work roles.[3] Certainly the principles summarized at the beginning of this chapter are as applicable to the individual level as they are to the departmental and team levels. How does one conceptualize work roles to ensure they include the elements of task variety, task identity, task significance, feedback, autonomy, and teamwork? Consider Figure 5–2.[4] Work can be typified into four main categories: (1) the operational core tasks that are directly related to the output of the organization; (2) support tasks that enable the core to operate efficiently over time (maintenance, quality, administrative); (3) coordination tasks, or the traditional managerial tasks that involve direction setting, decision making, and managing the tensions between change and stability; and (4) environmental tasks, the more strategic activities that link the system with the outside world. All four of these areas need consistent attention over time. Machine Theory split each of these tasks into isolated jobs or functions. Much of the Sociotechnical orientation and similar efforts have been aimed at combining some of these areas into a

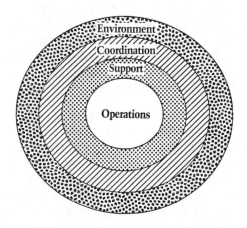

Figure 5–2
A Typology of Organizational Tasks

single role, and then providing even broader exposure through rotation into all four areas during the course of a person's career.

Structuring individual roles along these lines would mean:

- *There would be no rigid job descriptions.* Roles would be described with minimal critical specification to encourage the use of judgment and flexibility to do whatever is needed to get the needed result.
- *Roles would be enlarged* (greater variety of tasks) *and enriched* (more decision authority and autonomy). Operating and support functions would be combined wherever possible, creating self-sufficient operating units supported by lean staff groups.
- *Whenever appropriate, coordination and environmental tasks would also be built into individual roles at all levels.*
- *Rotation through different assignments during one's career* would not only develop multiple skills and greater

operational flexibility, but would also increase identification with the output rather than a job or special skill. It would also increase empathy for others in the system.

- *Teams would be a powerful mechanism* to balance the individual needs for variety and support with the task needs for consistency and dependability. Individual team members could trade off on different tasks and cross-train each other over time.

The above description is not a hypothetical one, but a description of what has typically happened in the HPOs. For example, let's recall the Packers — the upholstery manufacturing team that had such impressive results. The Packers' culture was admirable — one that was the envy of all who saw them in action. Now let's look at the work design guidelines that helped shape such a culture. The Packers' organization was committed to the following guidelines:

1. All work assignments will call for direct involvement in the core work of the unit.
2. The team will have within its membership the necessary skills to accomplish its task, with each member having the opportunity to specialize in some area.
3. There will be multiple routes for moving to higher levels of pay (operating, technical, coordinating).
4. No individual will have exclusive rights to tasks or equipment. Desirable and undesirable work will be shared among team members on a reasonable rotation.

These simple guidelines proved invaluable to the Packers and their management in testing staffing decisions. It was hard to drift too far from the organizational ideal when evaluating decisions against guidelines such as these.

A careful analysis of the work roles in your organization will probably reveal that managerial roles tend to incorporate many of these principles already. Other roles in the organization (operators, mechanics, secretaries, clerks, etc.) are usually lacking in several dimensions. Whatever your situation, resist the temptation to conclude that the Packer model or similar models are impractical for your organization. For example, there is probably no industry that is so set in its ways as the automobile industry. Assembly lines have been around from the early days of Henry Ford. Yet even members of this industry have been able to adapt their work along these lines with marvelous results.

In the late 1960s the management at Volvo in Sweden decided to restructure its factories to fit the characteristics of living systems.[5] It shelved its assembly-line thinking and reconceived the automobile production process to fit its employees' needs for task variety, task identity, task significance, feedback, autonomy, and team work. This resulted in a process that made the production equipment the tool, not the master. Today in the newer Volvo plants small work teams assemble an entire automobile using a curious shuttle vehicle, or carrier, to move to various locations where they install the motor, doors, tires, trunk, and so on. One version of the carrier can tilt the car 90 degrees, allowing team members to work in several spots at one time. The team programs the production process, is accountable for total results, and is highly autonomous in the daily operation. Along with this revolutionary breakthrough in its production process, Volvo has maintained both its high standards of quality and its popularity with consumers worldwide. Moreover, Volvo has been successful in creating a work environment in which employees feel like partners in the business. After years of skepticism, other auto makers are now recognizing the significance of the Volvo experience. Similar experiments are now underway at Ford and General Motors.

A Work Design Process

Having reviewed some points to consider when designing work at the departmental, team, and individual levels, let me now share one approach to illustrate how one might actually analyze a work flow to design a Pine Valley, a Packers team, or a Volvo plant. The following process is based on Sociotechnical principles. It is an approach for analytically examining the work tasks to be performed; the various social and technical factors influencing the work; and the knowledge, skills, information, and cooperation required to create high performance.

The steps in this design process are:

1. Draw out a detailed technical process flow tracing the flow of material or information from start to finish.
2. Identify the phases in which a noticeable change in the input occurs. These phases are the unit operations.
3. Determine where the key variances occur in the flow of each unit operation. A variance is a deviation from the norm. Variances may occur due to the state of the input to the unit operation, technical procedures or techniques, technical breakdowns, or human errors. List only those variances that have a major impact on the work flow.
4. Determine where the variances are controlled and by whom.
5. List the tasks that need to be performed to correct the variances.
6. Document the knowledge and skills that are required to perform the tasks.
7. Determine what information and cooperation are needed to perform the tasks effectively over time.

This approach collects the needed data for determining departmental, team, and individual role structures plus helps the designer assess the training and development needs. To illustrate how this process actually works, let's examine the printing shop that served as an example earlier for departmental boundary setting. First review the task flow on p. 137.

Step one is to lay out this process in a straight line.

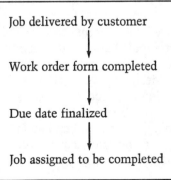

Job delivered by customer

↓

Work order form completed

↓

Due date finalized

↓

Job assigned to be completed

Step two is to identify the unit operations. You will recall that we broke the process into three unit operations: Job delivered by customer→Page layouts done, Printing completed→Errors corrected, and Job sorted/collated→Job picked up by customer.

Step three lists the variances that occur to hamper the ideal process flow.

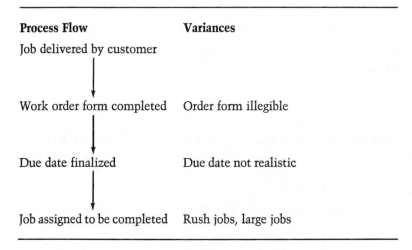

Process Flow	Variances
Job delivered by customer	
Work order form completed	Order form illegible
Due date finalized	Due date not realistic
Job assigned to be completed	Rush jobs, large jobs

Step four determines where the variances are controlled and by whom.

Process Flow	Variances	Controlled By
Job delivered by customer		
Work order form completed	Order form illegible	Supervisor A
Due date finalized	Due date not realistic	Supervisor A
Job assigned to be completed	Rush jobs, large jobs	Supervisor A

The key question in this step is whether or not variances are being controlled as near to their point of origin as possible. From this slice of the printing shop's work flow, we can see that the variances caused by the receiving clerk are being corrected by Supervisor A.

Step five asks us to list the tasks which need to be performed to correct the variances.

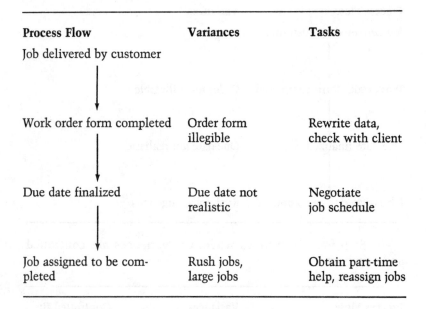

Process Flow	Variances	Tasks
Job delivered by customer		
Work order form completed	Order form illegible	Rewrite data, check with client
Due date finalized	Due date not realistic	Negotiate job schedule
Job assigned to be completed	Rush jobs, large jobs	Obtain part-time help, reassign jobs

Step six asks us to document the knowledge and skills which are required to perform the tasks.

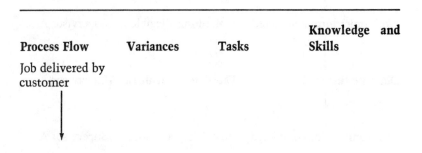

Process Flow	Variances	Tasks	Knowledge and Skills
Job delivered by customer			

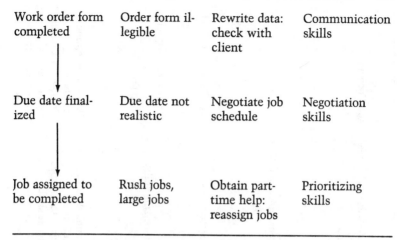

Work order form completed	Order form illegible	Rewrite data: check with client	Communication skills
Due date finalized	Due date not realistic	Negotiate job schedule	Negotiation skills
Job assigned to be completed	Rush jobs, large jobs	Obtain part-time help: reassign jobs	Prioritizing skills

Step seven helps us determine what information and cooperation are needed to perform the tasks effectively over time. This is where the desirability of a team structure can be assessed for the work situation.

Variances	Tasks	Knowledge and Skills	Information and Cooperation
Order form illegible	Rewrite data: check wtih client	Communication skills	
Due date not realistic	Negotiate job schedule	Negotiation skills	Total shop work load Shop output capacity Shop priorities Printers' accepting schedule
Rush jobs: large jobs	Obtain part-time help: reassign jobs	Prioritizing skills	

Process Flow	Variances	Tasks	Knowledge and Skills	Information and Cooperation
Job delivered by customer				
Work order form completed	Order form illegible	Rewrite data Check with client	Communication skills	
Due date finalized	Due date not realistic	Negotiate schedule	Negotiation skills	Total shop workload
Jobs assigned to be completed	Rush jobs Large jobs	Obtain part-time help Reassign jobs	Prioritizing skills	Shop output capacity Shop priorities
Page layouts done	Equipment breakdowns Layout errors	Fix equipment Redo layout	Troubleshooting equipment Repair techniques Layout skills	*Printers' accepting schedule *Troubleshooting and repair help *Share layout equipment

Process step	Problem/cause	Action	Skills/knowledge	Cooperation items
Printing completed Job checked for errors	Misaligned printer Poor inking Wrong ink colors	Align printer Reink or repair Repeat printing	Printer troubleshooting and repair Ink system functioning Printer operation	*Troubleshooting and repair help *Share redistributed jobs Job deadlines *Share printers
Job sorted/collated	Collator malfunction Lost pages	Repair collator Repeat printing	Collator troubleshooting and repair Printer operation	*Troubleshooting & repair *Share printers Quality of work output Performance trends Spending versus budget
Customer notified	Miscommunication	Apologize Smooth over	Communication skills Handling customer relations	
Job picked up by customer	Customer dissatisfied with final job	Understand problem Redo job Clarify shop capability	Listening skills Job deadlines	*Redoing a job (printers) Shop printing capability

*Identifies cooperation items.

Figure 5–3
An Example of the Work Design Process Applied to a Printing Shop.

If the designer had all of this information clearly laid out in some manner, it would be easier to:

- Restructure work roles to correct variances where they occur.
- Identify areas where employees were not prepared to handle the tasks and arrange for training and development.
- Determine whether a team structure would help performance and output.

In short, it would be possible to improve the work system to achieve greater self-sufficiency and high performance. Reflecting on a point made earlier in the Outside-In approach, the redesign of work at the basic task level is what frees up supervisors and managers to spend more of their time on boundary management of the environmental interfaces.

To give you a clearer picture of how this process works, see Figure 5–3, a detailed summary of the key work flow data for the printing shop. One would need to add to this data the analysis of who actually controls the variances in the present system to have a complete picture of the current process.

Although there are many ways to approach work design, the important thing to keep in mind is that high performers usually undergo a thorough analysis of their work process before making critical design decisions. The pure Sociotechnical analysis is more rigorous than the one I have presented here.[6] For some situations the added rigor is necessary. For others, processes like this one will yield the most important data needed to make the design decisions.

Conclusion

High performing organizations are characterized by structures that reinforce the qualities of living systems. Although this should seem natural, it is not. Centuries of organizing work based on Machine Theory have influenced our thinking about how to divide work. The principles and approaches outlined in this chapter have been helpful to many high performers by allowing them to harness the natural energy of their people against the tasks to be completed. The high performers have learned to design for results and self-sufficiency rather than for form and elaborate supervisory control. Their focus is on getting the work done right in the first place rather than detecting or controlling errors after they have been made. Often it is the rigorous design process itself that jolts members of the organization into a realization of how much better their performance could be.

Notes

1. E. L. Trist, "The evolution of socio-technical systems: A conceptual framework and an action research program," Ontario Quality of Working Life Centre, Issues in the Quality of Working Life Occasional Paper Number 2, June 1981); J. R. Hackman and G. R. Oldham, *Work redesign* (Reading, Mass.: Addison-Wesley, 1980).

2. E. J. Miller, "Technology, territory, and time: The internal differentiation of complex production systems," in W. A. Pasmore, and J. J. Sherwood, eds., *Sociotechnical systems: A sourcebook* (La Jolla, Calif.: University Associates, 1978), 96–119.

3. F. Herzberg, *Work and the nature of man* (Cleveland: World, 1966); F. Herzberg, "One more time: How do you motivate employees?" *Harvard Business Review* (January-February 1968):53–62; L. E. Davis and J. C. Taylor, *Design of jobs*, 2nd ed. (Santa Monica, Calif.: Goodyear, 1979); S. Srivastva, P. F. Salipante, Jr., T. G. Cummings, W. W. Notz, J. D. Bigelow, and J. A. Waters, *Job satisfaction and productivity* (Kent, Ohio: The Comparative Administration Research Institute, Kent State University Press, 1977).

4. F. E. Kast and J. E. Rosenzweig, *Organization and management: A systems approach*, 2nd ed. (New York: McGraw-Hill, 1974), 137–141.

5. P. G. Gyllenhammar, *People at work* (Reading, Mass.: Addison-Wesley, 1977); P. G. Gyllenhammar, "How Volvo adapts work to people," *Harvard Business Review* (July-August, 1977):102–113; N. M. Tichy and J. N. Nisberg, "When does work restructuring work? Organizational innovations at Volvo and GM," *Organizational Dynamics* (Summer 1976):63–80.

6. F. E. Emery and E. L. Trist, "Analytical model for sociotechnical systems," in W. A. Pasmore and J. J. Sherwood, eds. *Sociotechnical systems; A sourcebook* (La Jolla, Calif.: University Associates, 1978), 120–131; J. C. Taylor, "The human side of work: The socio-technical approach to work system design," *Personnel Review* (Summer 1975):17–22.

6

Managing Cultural Change

As is evident from the discussion in Chapters 4 and 5, the design process is an exhaustive undertaking. Unfortunately, designing how the organization *should* operate in the future doesn't always guarantee that it *will* operate that way. Some planners are disappointed with their organization's results when, after doing everything seemingly right in the design process, they neglect the process of managing the cultural change as the old system begins to implement the new design.

Once the organization's new design is agreed, what else do you have to worry about? Consider the following:

- No behaviors have actually changed yet.
- Some assumptions you have made in the design process are probably erroneous.
- Commitment to the new way of working together has yet to be tested under fire.

Addressing each of these points requires a focused and determined effort to monitor the cultural attributes that emerge as design implementation begins. Progress should be highlighted and reinforced; attempts to revert to the old way of doing things should be countered constructively and patiently; indicators that the new design isn't working should be studied and understood; adjustments should be made as necessary. Open Systems Theory describes for us the powerful forces of the steady state and warns us of the opposition it can provide to needed systems changes. Even changes that will prolong survival may be resisted in the attempt to preserve the equilibrium of the status quo.

For the initiators of change, this means that how they manage the implementation phase will determine to what extent the organization's culture actually evolves to the desired state. The actual culture will determine what the actual results of the system will be—whether they be worthy of the designation *high performance* or something less. You can rest assured that every new strategic or design decision will be tested by members of the system, particularly if the new direction goes against the established culture. How the organization's leaders respond to these tests will determine whether the old cultural practices are discarded or not.

The important point to remember about cultural change is that behaviors rarely change without a change in the underlying assumptions, values, and attitudes. Everyone brings their own organizational biases with them to the workplace. In both new organizational start-ups and existing systems renewal efforts, true cultural change does not occur until several individuals—a critical mass—have examined and changed their basic assumptions about organizations. These attitudes have usually been shaped over a period of years, either by the organization itself or by social conditioning before the organization's existence. One cannot change such attitudes overnight, but they can be influenced by an effective change strategy. As an example, consider how the processes of assessment and design might begin to have an impact on individuals' organizational attitudes. A systems assessment can explain why some valued aspects of the organization are not working effectively. By examining the conflict between their own organizational biases and the assessment data, the planners might be influenced to "unfreeze" their thinking and consider new possibilities. Similarly, the design process, by referring to sociotechnical guidelines and others' experiences with them, can constructively challenge the planners' view of how things ought to be. Both processes, therefore, can help individuals make more informed, conscious choices about their organizational assumptions and values. But the challenge still remains to act consistently with these new values. In the midst of the change process, it is natural to revert to old attitudes and habits whenever challenges arise or uncertainty exists.

This chapter describes how many of the HPOs have managed the cultural changes to be consistent with their design choices. I will describe what HPOs look like culturally, outline the most critical issues that determine the success or failure of achieving cultural change, and conclude by discussing some of the dynamics of backsliding, or how you can tell if you are falling off the pinnacle of high performance.

Cultural Attributes of HPOs

In addition to whatever their design attributes may be, most High Performance Organizations are characterized by a few critical cultural attributes. They are successful in the implementation stage because of the following factors:

1. *Strong, radical leaders.* Many of the High Performance Organizations have been led by individuals who refuse to be denied fulfillment of their sense of purpose or mission. Based on years of experience, these leaders develop a vision of what might be. They choose an organizational setting to pursue this vision — and pursue it with incredible determination. Most of these leaders elicit strong feelings of love and hate from those they work with. But most everyone agrees with the leaders' mission and finds it easy to overlook their idiosyncrasies because of the prospect of sharing in their dream.

   Such leaders know the environment and members of the system itself will exert incredible energy to maintain the status quo. They know this; they expect it; and they don't waver from their plan when it occurs. They recognize that a necessary part of their task is to influence others to examine their assumptions and values. Such determination and unwillingness to knuckle under to the system often earns them the label *radical*. Other labels that are applied to them by their supervisors, peers, and many subordinates include *uncooperative, unorthodox, egotistical, troublesome,* and *obstinate*. Their new approaches often threaten or worry many in the system. But these leaders don't care. The only thing that matters to them is to make their vision into reality. They have already calculated the odds against them and decided that their vision means more to them than being esteemed by the system. In time, most have been judged successful — in fact, many are recognized today as leaders of important breakthroughs. But I'm sure they felt lonely while much of the innovation was in progress. An important trend in many HPOs is that they start out with one strong leader at the helm, but see others emerge in the process.

2. *A clear vision of what needs to be done.* This vision sometimes arises out of a crisis that must be handled in order to save the business. But most of the time the vision of the true high performer comes from a mission statement that articulates the vision of the leader and others to the organization. Mission statements are still greatly misunderstood by many.

   Contrary to popular belief, the real effectiveness of missions is not in the *product* (i.e., the piece of paper or booklet), but in the *process*. The mission process in HPOs underscores their commitment to the value of consensus in the organization. It starts with a specific leadership group getting together and debating (often vehemently!) what it is they should be doing in their organization. This process of debating exposes similarities and differences of opinion and leads to a new definition of the ideal that is usually clearer and more demanding than any single perspective prior to the process. Clarity and conviction in the leadership team emerge from this process. The leaders become committed to making the mission a reality. The leadership team also spends a great deal of time enrolling large numbers of organization members to share the vision. Many discussions are held to make sure individuals at all levels of the organization have a common view of what's important.

This enrollment process usually goes even further; committed members of the system encourage others in related organizations to do whatever necessary — even suspend their standard operating procedures — in order to ensure fulfillment of the vision. In the few cases where this has happened, every critical person has worked committedly toward the mission's fulfillment — and breakthroughs have been achieved. This is a relatively rare phenomenon because not many understand the need or are willing to spend the time and energy to penetrate the entire network of resources to get consensus and real commitment to a mission. Without this clarity, however, daily decisions may be made that unconsciously undermine the original design intentions. Then, the design may not stand up in the heat of battle.

The real contribution of the mission statement is felt in the organization when it truly articulates the shared values of every person in that organization. These values represent the core beliefs — things that do not change easily. Such values can provide enormous security in times of stress and uncertainty by helping each individual determine which actions to take and which to avoid. Without clear values to provide such guidance, the tendency is to seek security and stability by fossilizing systems, procedures, rules, and practices.[1]

3. *A culture that meshes a strong concern for results with a strong concern for the individual.* This is a fascinating aspect of these systems. HPOs spend much time seemingly on a diversionary path from better results. They spend much time, attention, and money to give a clear signal that the needs of the employees are important organizational considerations. There are constant reminders about the importance of people — not just in public statements, but in steps to recognize individual needs, celebrations of accomplishments, decisions made based on considerations broader than just "the

numbers." One step many HPOs take is to change the titles and labels traditionally given to members of the system. The new titles become symbolic of the desired new culture. *Workers, nonmanagers, hourlies,* and *operators* become *associates* and *technicians.* Such steps are often a source of derision and taunting from other organizations: "... you people are softies;" "... running a country club instead of a business;" "... forgotten why you're in business;" and "... 'touchy-feely-culture.'" But the employee dedication and loyalty that come out are more than worth the investment. One thing I have observed about these cultures: to those who are in them, there is *no question* about their payoff. To those who have never been in one, there is *no answer* that will satisfy their skepticism.

4. *New work designs are pioneered.* It may seem obvious from the earlier chapters on the design process, but high performers experiment with new work designs that might relieve some of the perennial bureaucratic headaches that have existed for years. In general, they follow the principles of Sociotechnical Systems design. Work roles are expanded and optimized, delegation is practiced to an astonishing degree, and information is sent directly to the point of action. In these new designs work teams replace isolated individual specialists to complete a project, team coordinators replace managers on factory shifts, multifunctional teams or task forces take on major product initiatives, functional specialist networks support their members, rewards are based on actual contribution rather than position or seniority. All of these design changes have proven to be successful in a variety of situations. But I know there was a time when each was considered dangerous and irresponsible. HPOs are not afraid to experiment with the way they get their work done.

5. *The leadership is open to learn from others.* The leaders of HPOs very often are extremely open and responsive to new ideas from any source. They read profusely. And they spend a higher percentage of time than their peers

in attending formal training courses. They are slow to ridicule a new development — until they have had a chance to dig into it for themselves. They visit other operations to discover something new that might propel them closer to their vision. The intangible benefit that results from all this is the unspoken message that innovative, new ideas are welcome from anyone.

Another way this openness to learn is manifested is in the way the leaders react to bad news. The leaders are eager to have employees tell it like it is. They are not deluded about the current state of the operation. They recognize that there is a tendency to shield members of the hierarchy from unpleasant realities and they encourage their subordinates to speak up. They also go out of their way to know (firsthand) what's going on at the lab bench, on the shop floor, or in the field. While doing this, the leaders never lose sight of their vision. In fact, it is their absolute commitment to the vision that motivates them to uncover any conceivable factor that might prevent them from reaching their dream. When this attitude becomes a norm in the organization, employes at all levels focus on finding out what's breaking down in the system and fixing it.

6. *Challenge the impossible.* In each case, these organizations approach situations deemed impossible (based on past experience) and invent a way to break through them. This is one of the crucial differences between High Performance Organizations and others. People who work in HPOs actually believe they can make a difference in the way their organization performs. They feel free to try different (and often unconventional) methods to achieve a breakthrough.

Other organizations mean well, but are unwilling to risk failure by trying something revolutionary. They don't break through, but are able to point to many logi-cal reasons why they couldn't do it. Most of the time no one blames them. After all, nobody else was able to do it either. High Performance Organizations' commitment to find an answer far outweighs their fear of failure. This comes from what Roger Harrison has described as a focus on tasks and people more than on structure and power.[2] Because of this orientation, HPOs outmaneuver the typical bureaucratic constraints and often wind up doing the impossible. Doing so often stirs up the status quo (that's why it wasn't done before!) and may "ruffle the feathers" of outside groups.

The key to all this is the assumptions that leaders in the system make. Assumptions about individual trustworthiness, capability for self-management, environmental constraints, or personal status needs will to determine the degree of challenging or experimentation that will be evident in the system. The key question is, "What would it take to accomplish _____?" The usual statement in its place is, "We can't do that because _____." Without exception, the limitations to high performance are controlled by the leaders' assumptions of what is possible.

These cultural attributes fit neatly, or are congruent, with the design characteristics of living systems described in Chapters 4 and 5. As already discussed in the Organization Performance Model, high performance is the usual result of such a fit between design elements and cultural attributes.

Critical Issues for Managing Cultural Change: Don't Forget the Basics

Consider the following sports analogy: Moments before Super Bowl II, the great football coach Vince Lombardi motivated his Green Bay Packers for the biggest contest of their lives with the words, "Just hit, just run, just block, and just tackle."[3] Not exactly the stuff Hollywood scripts are made of! Yet this emphasis on the basics was what continually kept Lombardi's Packers ahead of their competitors. When it came down to the big play, the Packers executed to perfection.

Now let's translate the principle of Lombardi's pep talk to the subject of managing organizational culture change. I believe there are a few basic fundamentals that often spell the difference in creating high performance. Those who pay attention to the basics invariably win their competitive battles. Those who ignore these fundamentals usually end up paying dearly for their oversight. I call these fundamentals the *critical issues for managing cultural change*. They may not appear to be profound (neither is blocking and tackling), but in my experience they represent the difference between high performance and high frustration.

Develop a true commitment to the change. The leaders must be commited to *lead* the change effort. It is very rare that all key leaders in the organization will have identical points of view on *what* needs to be changed and *why* change is needed. Concerns, disagreements, and false expectations of the change effort, if not resolved early, will surface again during the course of implementing change. At best this is a distraction, but it could also cause the effort to fail. A deep, informed commitment grows out of dialogue, debate, and disagreement in which the strategy and tactics of change are questioned. If agreement can be reached after such questioning, it will most likely be a committed agreement. If leaders cannot agree, the chances of success are marginal anyway.

For example, a service organization had been conducting an organization redesign project for several years. After some initial progress in one department, the project momentum had stopped. The managing director was concerned. After some soul-searching with his top management team, the director began to understand that many of them were not supportive of the project and never had been! The director and one department head (where progress had been made) had pushed their dream past others' unspoken concerns. These concerns had festered through the years and were now killing the momentum. The top team held a series of meetings to explore what the residual concerns were and what the actual effects of the project would be on each department. The team was able to give full support to a modified plan that would still lead to high performance. With new leadership support, the change effort began to move ahead impressively.

The leaders aren't the only ones who need to lead, support, or implement change. A communication plan is needed to discuss the change effort with all those who will be affected by it.

It is important for these individuals to understand *what* will be different after the change and *why* the changes are needed to improve business results.

One plant manager I know made a personal visit to every work team in his plant to share the business situation facing them, explain how his vision of the organizational change effort would make them competitive again, and listen to any questions or concerns the employees had. This manager was not known as a softy by any means. He was a no-nonsense business person, but he recognized that he needed to build some understanding and commitment for the future plan among the employees. After weeks of discussions with all three work shifts, the plant manager had achieved his objective. Work design experiments were agreed to and began to progress nicely. Training in new skills commenced. Managers began filling new roles to facilitate the development of self-managing work teams.

Why the need for such broadscale commitment? There is an old saying that sums up nicely the issue at hand, *"Those convinced against their will are of the same opinion still."* Experience suggests that forced change will fail. Change imposed from the top produces compliance, not commitment. Once the external pressure to change eases (as it invariably does in a complex change effort requiring years to complete), the system will revert to those operating methods it knows best and truly values.

There is another important point relating to commitment: effectively managing employee expectations of the change effort. Too often in the attempt to share a common vision, managers inadvertently lead others to believe that "heaven on earth" is right around the corner. When things don't progress according to these expectations, a certain cynicism can creep into the system. *Management has gone back on its word* is a phrase that is often heard. Countering this phenomenon requires clearly spelling out what is meant and what is *not* meant by the organizational vision. It also requires sharing the uncertainties when they exist. Clear examples and rough timetables may be helpful in calibrating everyone's expectations. Changes in plans due to new developments also need to be shared forthrightly. I don't believe managers striving for high performance ever consciously break their promises. But they do occasionally say something other than what employees hear, or they change their plans based on new information. Penetrating communication is the key to managing different expectations.

I saw the wasteful effects of mismatched expectations in one manufacturing plant. Employees had been told from their first day on the job that their work groups would be self-managing "as soon as you can take on more responsibility." The plant mission stated that "decisions will be made at the lowest possible level." When I interviewed a cross-section of employees two years after the plant's start-up, I found that many felt they had been deceived by management. Not one work group was self-managing. Managers still made most of the day-to-day decisions. Each person admitted this was the best job she or he had ever had, but each was disturbed that certain promises hadn't been kept. Conversations with the plant's leaders revealed the following: "How could they expect to do all that in two years? Other plants have been at it for over five years and are just beginning." Clearly there were different ideas elicited by the phrases *self-management* and *decision making at the lowest possible level.* Management addressed the mismatched expectations. Reality and reason prevailed. The organization continued to make admirable progress and eventually reached "the promised land." Today there are no shift supervisors in the plant. Work teams are truly self-managing.

Develop High Performance skills. Because HPOs produce better results, we often assume they are easier to manage. Unfortunately this is not the case. Changes in organization design usually result in new (expanded, enriched, more complex, different) roles for all employees. This usually requires a high level of training, or at least more training than the previous system required, while carrying on the daily work. The High Performance Organizations I am familiar with have devoted a disproportionate amount of time (versus their peers) to training. A Procter & Gamble manufacturing survey a few years ago illustrated this best. The newer P&G innovative work systems spent approximately three times the number of hours in ongoing training situations as their older, traditional counterparts. I have seen similar patterns in other types of organizations as well. People are actively encouraged to learn and develop new perspectives and skills so as to be able to handle an ever-changing work load.

It may be useful to view this change effort as a start-up situation (which it is) and the individuals as "new hires" to be trained for new positions. Shortcut approaches, which attempt to minimize training, frequently "set up" the change effort to fail. Inadequate training will mean people aren't skilled to operate the new system. This yields poor results which may cause some to want to revert to what used to work. Such difficulties can be avoided with an up-front investment in preparing the people for the tasks to be accomplished.

For instance, the Slate Company was going through the throes of downsizing. A branch office was to be closed and some employees transferred to a nearby location. The only problem was that the office to be shut down had been operating under traditional bureaucratic work principles. The neighboring office had been successfully practicing an innovative work system with clerical work teams and fewer supervisors. It also had the newest office technology. Management was concerned about the transition for those members moving from the old to the new office. After consulting with an organizational specialist, a plan was devised to train the transferees on the social and technical skills required in the new office. A two-week training program was designed for all transferees. At the end of the program management observed an unusually smooth transition. Even the most resistant individuals were willing to give teamwork a try. All were proficient in the new office technology. After a few months it was hard to tell the transferees from those who had opened up the office.

Compare the Slate Company's experience with what organizations more typically do in a similar situation. There is never time to pull employees off the job for such training, consequently the organization suffers for months, even years, because of poor joining up, long adjustment periods, high turnover, or similar maladies.

Dedicate sufficient resources to manage cultural change. The change effort represents new tasks that have to be managed and carried out. It follows logically that key individuals must have responsibility (and the time!) to manage the change in culture. Thus line and staff resources must be made available to do the needed work. Tasks may have to be shifted to allow key individuals to spend time moving the old culture to levels of high performance. Some additional staff resources may also be needed (technologist, strategic planner, organizational consultant, human resources specialist, etc.) to ensure success. Those who ignore this reality and try to approach the situation as if it were business as usual end up paying a high price.

For example, a subsidiary of a well-known oil company was trying to achieve better organizational performance. A highly competitive business situation had threatened the very existence of the organization. Competitors had recently introduced superior products at lower costs. The subsidiary's growth and profitability were at a standstill. Clearly it needed to address some key strategic questions while it continued to battle daily pressures. An outside consultant was brought in to assist with the initial planning. After a couple of days, the consultant recommended the subsidiary increase its staff by one or two people to allow some of the leaders to spend more time planning and managing the changes required for high performance. The CEO felt this was impractical and assigned one of his financial managers to be the organizational project manager in addition to his normal duties. Everything started off fine. The CEO and his team went through a strategic planning process that pinpointed what the organization would need to do to regain a competitive advantage in the next five years. The subsidiary's strategy won high praise from the parent company's top management. The blueprint was in place for a return to prosperity.

In time, the business pressures became so great that everyone's attention was riveted to the daily work load. Debugging existing products proved to be a full-time job for the research and development people who were supposed to be developing a new breakthrough product. Increasing immediate sales contracts monopolized the thinking of those who were supposed to be developing new markets. The number of short-term productivity activities prevented the CEO from mapping out fundamental structural changes that would forever improve productivity. Numerous daily decisions had to be made, thus driving out time for considering strategic issues. The finance manager/organization project leader was desperately needed to determine the financial implications of a host of issues that varied each day. The organizational project slowly slipped into the background. The subsidiary continues to struggle to this day.

Adequate resources provide the organization with the necessary slack to manage the daily business *and* facilitate the longer term improvements. In the short term, such slack may prove to be the critical difference between shifting the system to high performance or burning up much energy without affecting true systems change.

Even if one has the right resources in place today, this is not always enough to ensure cultural change. Stability of personnel is also needed over time to lead and support large systems change. A broad base of resources is essential to provide this leadership and support because some key individuals will *always* move out of the system before the change is completed. The importance of this was illustrated in one department that was involved in developing self-managing work teams. At the outset of the project each team had one strong, natural leader who made things happen. The plan was to gradually rotate leadership responsibilities so that many leaders were developed. Through the next couple of years the teams pursued their rotation of leaders even though there was no immediate need to do so. The natural leaders stepped aside and served as consultants to their successors. Four years later, as fate would have it, all three of the original leaders were transferred simultaneously to other departments. The change effort was at a crucial stage, but the department's performance never wavered. The other leaders picked up the slack and kept the operation at the top of the pack.

Such stability and continuity of resources to sustain cultural change don't just happen. They have to be planned and managed in order to occur through the life of the project.

Overcome old habits. Most people are used to narrowly defined jobs (Machine Theory). Their habits may be hard to change. This does not necessarily mean they prefer the old way of doing things (most who have gone through the transition prefer high performance). It simply means they are more comfortable with familiar arrangements. Habits change when the system clearly signals it is important to do so. The key signals everyone watches are pay, promotion, and to what things leaders pay attention. These elements are all inseparably linked to the work that is done. Any changes in work design must also be accompanied by reinforcing changes in these three areas. Pay and promotion may seem obvious as ways of reinforcing new behaviors, but what about what the leader pays attention to? How can this help overcome old habits?

A new CEO was brought into one technical organization to affect major changes in the way the company operated. His predecessors had spent most of their time studying technical proposals and following up on technical projects. The managers were mostly engineers who had strong technical skills. At the time, however, the organization was suffering. Changes in the environment were engulfing it. Interfaces had seriously broken down and many projects had suffered as a result. The human resource development program had degenerated and was almost non-existent. New employees were noticeably less prepared for their work than older employees. The CEO tried to put more balance into the daily priorities. Because of the size of the organization, he chose to spend most of his time with his top team or in individual reviews with each of them. The primary intervention made by this CEO was in drawing up the agenda for each meeting. Rather than being dominated by technical items, two-thirds of each agenda was devoted to human resources and organizational change issues. For instance, the technical projects were reviewed with each department head *after* the agenda items about creating development plans for each of their subordinates, strategic planning, and interface improvements with outside contacts. As a result of these many discussions with each department head, people development accelerated as did organizational redesign efforts and improved interfaces with suppliers and customers. Within two years the performance of the company had improved dramatically in all respects — technically as well as in the organizational arenas. The CEO's major tool for affecting such change? The things he paid attention to when talking to others.

New work roles also have an impact on individuals' need for information. Information systems must be studied and changed to permit changes in who does what. A failure to redesign the information system may result in the continuation of old work habits. ("Others can't do this job, they don't know what's going on. I'll continue doing it my way.") This is one area that usually challenges management's creativity and willingness to take risks. The normal concerns about employee trustworthiness and security typically lead to information being shared on a need-to-know basis. There is no inconsistency with a need-to-know policy and sharing information for high performance. The critical change that must occur, however, is an accurate redefinition of who needs to know what in order to complete the given work tasks.

Manage the environment. All too often organizations initiate internal change efforts without assessing what impact these changes will have on outsiders who are critical to the organization's success. This is another symptom of Internal Myopia. The change strategy, expectations, and tracking mechanisms need to be agreed on with key external groups (hierarchy, related departments, customers) in the environment. Failure to do so may risk interference from these outsiders in terms of overcontrol or lack of support. Either outcome could terminate the project. Even if the change effort succeeds, failure to manage the environment may prevent further spreading of a good thing — and shortchange the potential benefit to the parent organization or society.

One high performer, Brock Industries, had a particularly rough time with members of its business environment. Its management team had done an extensive investigation of high performance and had used a thorough design process as it started up. The managers were excited by the culture that was emerging and the results that were making it a high performer in its early days. But it soon began receiving signals from those in its environment that it was not being appreciated despite its business results. Visitors to Brock came away dismayed by the organizational jargon and apparent lack of concern about results ("All they talk about there is meeting people's needs or their latest organizational gizmo"). Contacts with other departments at headquarters further reinforced this culture shock.

A period came when Brock's business results slipped and the critics became quite vocal everywhere. Other organizations wanted nothing to do with Brock's business methods. It was considered unreliable as a source for further business expansion. Luckily for Brock, it was assigned a new leader who began working on the environmental interfaces. Brock managers began to describe what they were doing in normal business terminology. Every organizational experiment was framed by the business need that had caused its creation and the improved results it was delivering to the business. Greater sensitivity was shown toward headquarters and culture shock was minimized even though the two cultures remained quite different. In short, by carefully managing its environment Brock turned its image around, achieved even better business results, and became recognized as a high performer by those who had previously been its skeptics. All of this culminated in headquarters choosing Brock as the site for the latest expansion project. Brock's efficiency, productivity, innovation, and flexibility have made it a model for others to follow.

Many projects have also failed because of the so-called test cell syndrome, which means a situation in which the leadership is not in agreement on the *what* or *why* of the change, but agrees to let one group be a test cell to see if the recommended change works. If it does work, the agreement is to spread the change further. If it doesn't, the idea is forgotten. If a hostile environment believes it can influence such a go-no go decision, it will find ways to discredit the experiment and terminate it. Test cells may be helpful, *if* leaders are committed to the change and agree that the purpose of the test cell is to yield results and experience that can be improved on *when* (not *if*) the change moves to other areas.

Managing these critical issues while exhibiting the cultural characteristics of high performance and producing today's business results is an enormous challenge. The classic volume in this series, *Organizational Transitions: Managing Complex Change* by Beckhard and Harris,[4] is an excellent resource for those contemplating such an undertaking.

The Dynamics of Backsliding

There is another dimension to the critical issue of managing cultural change for high performance. Sometimes it isn't even enough to achieve the desired culture in the short term. Once you have reached the pinnacle of high performance, there are numerous gravitational forces that may attempt to pull you back down. Members of HPOs are always wary of backsliding into old ways as time passes.

The easiest way to backslide is to make a change in key leadership positions in the midst of or at the conclusion of the change effort. It's not just the change of leaders that is the problem. Backsliding occurs when the new leaders have a fundamental opposing philosophy to the changes that have been initiated. In such situations, the new leaders exhibit some or all of the following symptoms:

- They don't accept the existing mission and operating principles and they express no personal vision to replace them. Their approach to the business is the no-nonsense, tried and true way.
- An emphasis on hard number results (shorter term, more predictable, and safer) replaces the mission or vision.
- There is a tightening up on the delegation practices. Things must be checked and approved. It is assumed the levels below are going to make mistakes and must be closely supervised.
- The concern for people becomes hollow. Daily behavior begins to show an insensitivity to people's needs. There may even be labeling of the former culture's leaders as soft.
- Work structures revolve primarily around chains of command and hierarchy. New ways of organizing work are frowned upon.
- The Not Invented Here (NIH) syndrome begins to set in. The leaders believe they have more experience and knowledge than others in the system. There is little chance to have an impact on their thinking with new ideas.
- The realm of possibility is limited to the set of assumptions based on past experience. People stick with what has worked in the past for fear of falling short with an experiment. Methods and procedures are adapted only

when a real crisis clearly indicates the old ways won't work.

- Training is pretty much limited to on-the-job training because there is so much to do to get today's results accomplished.
- The need-to-know information policy is reinstituted out of concerns for security. A filtering of information occurs until the top and bottom of the system have very different perceptions.

Each of these symptoms has a very powerful rationale for why it has worked or may be needed. Taken in their totality, however, they serve to destroy High Performance Organizations.

Is there a practical way to get around this dilemma? Perhaps the following actual case study will serve as a useful model for how one may need to proceed to avoid backsliding by really changing the dominant assumptions and values of those in the system.

A Procter & Gamble manufacturing director became convinced of the need for High Performance Organizations in his plants. Prior to his promotion, he himself had been through an exhilarating experience of designing and starting up such an organization. He tried to sell his dream to the remaining plants. They weren't interested. After months of debates and philosophical tugs-of-war, the director dropped the subject. It was obvious to him that these other plants did not want and would be unable to develop an HPO culture. Moreover, organizations outside of manufacturing were also exhibiting considerable hostility toward the prospect of new cultures springing up in every plant. This would be disruptive and irresponsible, they said. It was clear to the manufacturing director that his assumptions were not in line with those around him. He felt he had two choices to improve things. He could either change the people (Plan A), or change their assumptions and values (Plan B).

This manager decided on Plan B. He selected key leaders in each of his plants and formed them into a group to be trained in the theories, tools, and practices of developing High Performance Organizations. The training was not to be a panacea or brainwashing program. Rather, it explored in depth what High Performance

Organizations are all about and how one might develop them. In time, these managers came to value such systems. They weren't all wild-eyed radicals, but they all did understand, appreciate, and develop some skills in managing HPO cultures. Given this new conviction, their behaviors and values became aligned to achieve high performance.

The training group not only learned a lot themselves, they were assigned to train the next generation of leaders in the same material. As time went on, each major assignment was filled by a graduate of one of these training groups. All plant managers and key operating heads were alumni of the training groups. Some even transferred and held responsible positions in some of the key interface organizations. The message had become clear: anyone who wanted to progress in the organization had to get a healthy dose of this training!

With the key leaders now in position, the manufacturing director tried again to institute HPOs. This time the response was different. Each plant, though unwilling to become a clone of their cousin, had strong interest in pursuing a change program that would make it more effective. Work began at each location. The general targets were the same, but the paths traveled to reach the target varied greatly from plant to plant. However, each plant was making positive progress and was excited about *"our* change effort."

Now, about ten years after Plan B was begun, this manufacturing director has been promoted again (confounding those who maintain that risk taking doesn't pay) — and with good reason. His plants are all doing well — and are frequently touted as models for others to follow. But most importantly, he has left in place a talented management group that is able to sustain what he started.

Backsliding doesn't always begin at the top, however. You will remember I said at the beginning of this chapter that every new strategic or design decision will be tested by members of the system. How the organization's leaders respond to the system's tests can either stop backsliding or increase its momentum.

An example of a system's test is a manufacturing plant that was in its sixth year of operating with an innovative work system. One of the cornerstones of this system was a job rotation system that required individuals to learn different parts of the operation over time. After five years, the system had demonstrated tremendous flexibility because people could help out (skillfully) in many areas. The corollary to the rotation practice was the guideline that forbade any person from settling into one job and staying there. In the sixth year a few individuals refused to rotate out of their specialist assignments. Management recognized that if they compromised this feature of the work system, then others would settle into their favorite assignments and the flexibility would slowly ebb away. Accordingly, those who refused to rotate were terminated. After that no one questioned whether the leaders were serious about rotation.

Similarly, another manufacturing team was being groomed for self-management. The team had been functioning without a shift supervisor for about a year. As the team approached the week of the midnight, or graveyard, shift, its coordinator and best technologist were both going to be on vacation. Senior management's assumption was the team would require a manager to keep things under control. Luckily, the department managers recognized that this situation was a test of their commitment to self-management. One of the managers led a frank discussion in the team meeting prior to the first midnight shift. The team felt very strongly that it could handle things without additional help. Together with the manager, the team agreed to work out its own problems during the week. Only if results were obviously bad would the manager join them for the rest of the week.

The team proved itself that week. Despite two of its top performers being out, it had a near-record week in all results areas. There were no personnel problems. Upon their return, the two stars were jokingly told the team would continue to do well in spite of, not because of them. Everyone in the department had worked together to avoid backsliding to a situation where the team was dependent on management supervision to get acceptable results.

In an effort to move decision making closer to the action, one general manager at another company created a project team comprised of the various disciplines (sales, manufacturing, marketing, product development, finance, etc.) who could have an impact on the total results of the product they produced. The team was told to take ownership of the product's destiny. After months of planning and testing, the team had a new marketing idea that they felt had great potential. They shared it with the general manager and his reaction was emphatically negative. "That's one of the dumbest ideas I've ever heard," was his delicate response. Many team members were depressed. Under the old culture, what the boss said was the final word. But the team leader refused to let the team backslide into the old work habit. He encouraged the group to run some additional tests and to sample the idea with actual consumers. The tests were run and continued to show great promise. After several months the proposal was forwarded again. This time the market data were too much for even the skeptical general manager to ignore. The marketing idea was implemented and has continued to build the business ever since.

What each of these backsliding vignettes illustrates is the importance of the blocking and tackling fundamentals we discussed earlier. There is little chance of backsliding when:

- Strong leaders throughout the system are deeply committed to a vision of the future.
- Required values and skills for high performance are broadly distributed among the people involved.
- Each test of organizational resolve is managed by principle, not mere expediency.
- Environmental support is cultivated through skillful, sensitive interactions.

Conclusion

This chapter has explored some keys to managing cultural change for high performance. These are not theoretical hypotheses. They reflect the actual experiences of many who have been through these trying situations. These experiences suggest the highest performance occurs when (1) values and attitudes are congruent with business and cultural objectives and (2) the behaviors of organizational members are aligned appropriately with these values. Where other dynamics have existed, there have often been good, solid results — but not high performance.

Once you reach the point of implementing your strategy and design for high performance, it is prudent to evaluate the actual dynamics in your organization against the profile described here. If your organization looks like and feels like an HPO and addresses each of the critical issues for managing cultural change based on principle, then backsliding will be arrested and the emerging culture will live up to its design specifications. The results will confirm you as a high performer.

Notes

1. I am indebted to Dr. Stephen R. Covey for this important insight.

2. R. Harrison, "Understanding your organization's character," in J. E. Jones and J. W. Pfeiffer, eds., *The 1975 annual handbook for group facilitators* (La Jolla, Calif.: University Associates, 1975), 199–209; R. Harrison, "Understanding your organization's culture," unpublished manuscript, 1986.

3. J. Kramer, *Instant replay* (New York: The New American Library, 1968), 230–231.

4. R. Beckhard and R. T. Harris, *Organizational transitions: Managing complex change*, 2nd ed. (Reading, Mass.: Addison-Wesley, 1987).

7

Design Renewal: A Challenge to All

It is ironic that the concluding chapter in this book addresses the topic of renewal. I'm sure the last thing on your mind right now is starting over. This is not unlike the feelings one has after going through a comprehensive design or redesign process. And that is precisely why I have chosen to discuss this subject as my parting shot.

Consider for a moment what the following have in common:

- The sundial.
- The icebox.
- The slide rule.

All three used to fill a meaningful role in mainstream society. How else was one supposed to tell time, keep perishable foods in good condition, or perform complicated mathematical computations? Today all three are veritable dinosaurs. They (and a host of other products) may soon be joined by the typewriter — assuming that computers and word processors continue their meteoric rise. Those organizations who based their livelihood solely on these products have no doubt moved along the path of obsolescence. This manifestation of Internal Myopia (product obsolescence) is guaranteed to lead to business shortfalls in a changing environment.

Maginot Lines in Management

The same myopia can distort management's vision about work processes and organization design. Methods of operation also can become so rigid as to make the organization uncompetitive. Consider the following example:

At the conclusion of World War I the French Army High Command constructed a series of large fortifications linked by underground passages along the Franco-German border of the Saarland. This chain of fortifications became known as the *Maginot Line*. It was originally constructed to provide protection during mobilization and to aid the armies in wartime maneuvers. In time, however, the French population and the Army High Command came to view the Maginot Line as an insurmountable barrier. A disproportionate number of French troops were deployed along the line as Nazi Germany began its march into World War II. The French strategy was to fight a defensive war and the Maginot Line was their tool for engaging the enemy at the border. The only problem was the Germans changed the border by invading the Benelux countries and going *around* the Maginot Line. Set in concrete facing eastward, the mighty cannons were useless as the blitzkrieg came from the north and west! France was toppled in a matter of weeks.

Now let's consider some business lessons to be learned from this war story. Managers often hide behind their own Maginot Lines, ascribing larger-than-life capabilities to their management and organizational tools. These tools and structures frequently are set in concrete, defying anyone to move or alter them. Machine Theory has been soundly condemned through the course of this book, but it once was an organizational innovation that surpassed anything used previously. Machine Theory has become obsolete, like the sundial, because the competitive world and people's expectations of their work have changed dramatically in the past two centuries.

Here are some examples of today's Maginot Lines:

- SONY Corporation's reliance on patent laws to protect its revolutionary Beta home video recorder technology. VHS competitors have outflanked SONY.
- ITT's top-down management style (epitomized by CEO Harold Geneen) during a period of enormous growth and expansion.
- Procter & Gamble's tried-and-true product test marketing procedures that, until recently, took two to three years to complete. The procedures were followed even though competition began (and continued) to preempt P&G's national rollouts with faster and riskier methods.
- Upper management's insistence in many companies that annual performance reviews be conducted even though employee feedback frequently indicates they accomplish very little.
- The administrative clerk in one department who re-copied data from computer printouts to the hand-recorded forms he had used (successfully) for years before computers were around.
- The designers who failed to question the effectiveness of a compensation system that was proving to be unwieldy and divisive to the work force. Defenders of the system were excited about using a new concept in compensation that had never been tried before.
- The manufacturing plant that was proud and protective of its new innovative organization design despite the fact that turnover was 30 percent and costs were not competitive with a major Japanese rival.

As these examples show, rigidity and myopia may be found in all kinds of work systems — whether they be new or old. This symptom of Internal Myopia (organizational obsolescence) can lead to work processes that are unable to produce or sustain high performance in a changing environment. The emergence of Japan Inc. is sufficient reminder of how powerful an effective work process can be. It is generally acknowledged that few Japanese products represent technological discontinuities versus competition. What the Japanese companies typically offer the consumer is a very good product of superior quality and relatively low cost. Quality and cost are indicators of an effective work process.

Why High Performance Organizations Are Vulnerable

I maintain that High Performance Organizations can be even more vulnerable to pressures for maintaining the status quo and organizational rigidity than others. This is because they have exerted so much energy to give birth to and sustain the life of their organizational structures that they find it harder than others to terminate them when the business situation requires it. In this respect the cultures developed in HPOs can be both a blessing and a curse. We have already discussed how productive high performance work cultures can be. But they can also be overly sensitive and rigid to change. In this way HPOs can overestimate how good they really are just like the French High Command overestimated the capability of the Maginot Line.

Consider, for example, the case of the Westfall Plant, a large manufacturing organization in the midst of rapid environmental change in the early 1980s. The plant manager and his leadership team went through an exhaustive strategic planning and organization design process. After months of work, the plant had developed a new strategy and some organization design improvements aimed at achieving high performance. The implementation stage proceeded well, and in the ensuing eighteen months the plant became recognized as an HPO.

The leadership team had agreed to reassess the strategy's appropriateness from time to time. They now felt obligated to do this, even though they were skeptical that any significant changes would be needed. While this reassessment was being planned, the plant manager was suddenly transferred. The new plant manager had not participated in any of the previous strategic work. This turn of events shed a new light on things. The strategic reassessment would now provide an excellent mechanism for bringing the new leader on board. The team members carefully analyzed the results and state of development for their organizations. The new plant manager canvassed many of the plant's interface groups to learn about the external challenges and opportunities. When all the data were shared in the team, they showed the plant's environmental situation had subtly shifted in some ways that would have dramatic repercussions on Westfall in the next five years. In fact, the current plant strategy was already becoming obsolete. A new strategy emerged that provided a good fit with the changing environmental needs. Westfall adjusted itself to accomplish these new priorities and continued to be a high performer. Remember that before the change in plant managers, the leadership team had assumed the old strategy was still valid and that the environmental changes were insignificant!

Perhaps the clearest example in recent years of this phenomenon is the sad experience of People Express Airlines. This organization achieved something unprecedented in corporate history — it earned over $1 billion in only its fifth year of operation. As has been widely reported, there was a creative culture established at People Express that led to this high performance. Yet it fell off the pinnacle, in part, because CEO Don Burr and other top managers refused to consider changing aspects of their organization's design and culture, even though the company doubled in size almost overnight.[1] What worked well before no longer fit the new business situation at People Express. The renowned power struggle at Apple Computer between CEO and co-founder Steven Jobs and president John Scully was of a similar nature. Scully maintained that Apple would have to operate differently in a more competitive environment; Jobs resisted for fear of what change would do to the organization's culture.[2] Companies like Exxon, IBM, Johnson & Johnson, and Procter & Gamble are just as vulnerable to these dynamics because of their corporate cultures and traditions. Because these cultures have served their masters so well in the past, there is great reluctance to challenge their validity for the future. If major environmental shifts should occur, however, even these giants could be trapped like the makers of sundials, iceboxes, slide rules, or the French High Command.

What can high performers do to prevent such "hardening of the arteries"?

Nurturing the Capability for Renewal

There are four suggestions I would make to any organization attempting to renew its products and methods of operation. Let me introduce the first with another analogy.

Across the Firth of Forth, a large inlet on the east coast of Scotland, stands a steel bridge connecting a busy motorway between Edinburgh and Dundee. Shortly after this bridge was inaugurated, it was determined that it must be painted to prevent rust and other deterioration that would result from the area's rainy climate. A painting crew was commissioned to do the job. After months of work (it's a *long* bridge!) the crew finally completed its task. Upon further inspection, however, officials found that nature's deterioration had begun again at the starting point. The crew returned to paint and thus began a cycle that continues to this day. The painting is no sooner done than it must be started again.

My first suggestion to organizations wishing to renew themselves is to *recognize that organization designing, like painting the Firth of Forth Bridge, is never done.* Particularly in our age of rapid environmental change, the half life of organizational interventions will continue to shrink. Designing organizations should be an iterative process, one that constantly determines what the business situation and business strategy require and then adjusts organization design elements so that higher performance will be the outcome.

Second, *constantly monitor events in the outside world at least as rigorously as internal events.* Internal Myopia is a dreaded disease! The Outside-In approach is one way of ensuring that critical external interface tasks are institutionalized and thereby handled with the same devotion as the more immediate core tasks. Most important of all the interface tasks is to develop an effective positive feedback loop that monitors how the environment values your purpose and output. Sundials gave way to mechanical timepieces. Iceboxes gave way to refrigerators. Slide rules gave way to pocket calculators. Each of these newer innovations are in turn giving way to advanced versions of fulfilling the same basic needs. Monitoring the environment will not change these trends, but it will allow the high perfomer to anticipate the change and to lead and manage it rather than the opposite. In the words of a former Procter & Gamble CEO commenting years ago on the potential of a new technology, "This sort of thing could severely hurt our business, but if it does, let us be the ones who do it!"

Third, *pledge your allegiance to organizational principles, not methods.* I stated in the preface that the principles in this book are universally applicable to any organization. The same does not hold true for the specific methods reviewed here. Open Systems Theory, Sociotechnical principles, and the processes of organization assessment and design are the anchors on which to hold. Specific models, checklists, and procedures should (and must) be modified as circumstances vary. Most organizations that are resistant to renewal efforts fall into the trap of protecting methodologies instead of adhering to principles.

An example of this was brought home to me in a meeting with a senior P&G executive and some middle managers. The meeting was called to review a preliminary proposal for restructuring a part of one organization. One middle manager's reaction to the proposal was, "That might undermine the brand management system!" Brand management, which was invented by P&G in the 1930s, has been a marvelous tool for the company and has been a source of great pride through the years. The senior executive replied calmly, "Maybe it will, but let's get clear about the *principles* to be achieved by the change and then see if the brand management structure, or anything else, is as important as the principles."

This is real wisdom. Once you are clear about the principles and strategic elements to be achieved in any organizational change, hold up the following items for scrutiny:

- Job descriptions.
- Team structures.
- Reporting relationships.
- Compensation systems.
- Hiring procedures.
- Information practices.
- Decision-making prerogatives.
- Norms or habits.

If any of these are more important than the strategic principles, then don't abandon them. In my experience, this will seldom be the case!

Finally, *maintain an active assessment process regardless of the organization's state of health.* Assessment must precede design just as diagnosis must precede prescription. One cannot judge the need for adjusting design elements without an assessment of what is out of fit. Whether one uses the OP Model or some other approach, the key point is to constantly review the business results with the business situation. It would be healthy to ask the following questions periodically:

- How well are our products and services being accepted by the customer?
- Is our financial growth and profitability in line with our expectations?
- Are there continuous improvements being made in our products/services?
- Are we seeing greater levels of innovation?
- Is productivity improving constantly?
- Do we experience continuous work process improvements?
- Do employees feel a greater sense of ownership in the company's fortunes than in the past?

Even the best High Performance Organizations cannot answer "yes" to each of these questions. If the answer is "no," ask the question, "Why?" That's all it takes to begin the assessment process.

Conclusion: The Need for a Vision of High Performance

High Performance Organizations are visionary and purposeful, not limited by maladies such as Internal Myopia. Being visionary does not automatically guarantee you will be always visionary however! High performance is a phenomenon that must be renewed in light of an ever-changing business environment. I have presented four suggestions to organizations who seek renewal:

- Recognize that designing organizations is a task that is never done.
- Constantly monitor developments in the external world and institutionalize interface tasks.
- Rely on principles, not methods or procedures, to determine if change is needed.
- Assess your performance versus the business situation even when you don't think it's necessary.

Maintaining skill and perspective in these four areas will allow you to see the world as it is, not as you think it is. In other words, these steps can help you maintain clear vision about your environment. The ability to design and develop High Performance Organizations is directly related to such vision because vision is required to:

- See your world as it is.
- See exactly what high performance would look like in your situation.
- See what specific steps might be taken to transform your present organization into a high performer.
- Stay on course when managing the cultural changes in the face of opposition.
- See when renewal is needed to maintain high performance over time.

Hopefully the material presented here has helped you examine some of your basic assumptions, values, and visions of what life should be like in organizations. Having labored at length to discuss the process of designing organizations for high performance, let me conclude by inviting you to recall some of the slogans used throughout the book to highlight the key points. Compare your vision now to what it was when you first started reading Chapter 1.

1. *"The fish only knows it lives in water after it is already on the river bank."* At this point you should be neither

oblivious to nor puzzled by the world of organizations in which you live.

2. *"What you look at is what you see."* You should be able to see more clearly exactly what makes your organization function the way it does. You recognize the organization is not just the bottom line, or technology, or people, or the structure. As the OP Model illustrates, the organization is a system of cause-and-effect relationships involving many elements to produce its output or bottom line.

3. *"What theory you use determines what you look for."* Hopefully, by the end of Chapter 2 you have discarded any residual vestiges you had of Machine Theory thinking. Viewing organizations as living, open systems is mind-expanding and liberating. It answers many of the questions and repairs much of the damage created by the bureaucratic model.

4. *"All organizations are perfectly designed to get the results they get."* The processes of assessment and design enable you to see why this statement is true and provide you the means to develop organizations capable of high performance.

5. *"Just block and just tackle."* At some point all great strategies must degenerate into work — the daily work in the trenches. Flawless execution of the basics in the mold of Lombardi's Green Bay Packers is required when managing cultural change to achieve high performance. Managing the cultural changes is what truly brings the visions of design into reality.

6. *"Don't hide behind your Maginot Lines!"* No organization, HPO or otherwise, is infallible. Today's high performers can backslide all too easily because of some internal flaws that grow into unwieldy problems or because of environmental changes that make today's methodologies outmoded. Renewal is required for those who will be the survivors and high performers of tomorrow.

High Performance Organizations operate with these six realities in mind. They have developed the capacity to engage in organizational planning and development while also running the current operation with excellent results. And they do all of this while nurturing a work climate that enhances the feelings of self-worth of the individuals who work in them. HPOs operate effectively in many arenas. This is the hidden side of high performance — the ability to get more things done with the same resources.

To get the most from your resources is the challenge of high performance. This book has aimed to provide ways of thinking about HPOs and some principles and techniques that would enable the manager or practitioner to take up this challenge. There is nothing mandatory about any of this. It remains a matter of choice. In the words of Dr. W. Edwards Deming, speaking in his seminars on methods for management of productivity and quality, "There's no law that says anybody has to improve. It's all voluntary. It's only a matter of survival."

Notes

1. "Many travelers gripe about People Express, citing overbooking," *The Wall Street Journal* (May 19, 1986); "Growing pains at People Express," *Business Week* (January 28, 1985):90–91; "Up, up and away? Expansion is threatening the humane culture at People Express," *Business Week* (November 25, 1985):80–94.

2. "Behind the fall of Steve Jobs," *Fortune* (August 5, 1985): 20–24.

References

Baker, F. *Organizational systems: General systems approaches to complex organizations.* Homewood, Ill.: Irwin, 1973.

Barrett, J. H. *Individual goals and organizational objectives: a study of integration mechanisms.* Ann Arbor, Mich.: Institute for Social Research, 1970.

Beckhard, R., and R. T. Harris. *Organizational transitions: Managing complex change.* 2nd ed. Reading, Mass.: Addison-Wesley, 1987.

Bennis, W. G., K. D. Benne, R. Chin, and K. E. Corey, eds. *The planning of change.* 3rd ed. New York: Holt, Rinehart and Winston, 1976.

Boulding, K. E. "General systems theory: The skeleton of science." *General Systems.* Yearbook of the Society for the Advancement of General System Theory, 1:11–17.

Bradburn, N. M., S. Sudman, and associates. *Improving interview method and questionnaire design.* San Francisco: Jossey-Bass, 1979.

Buckley, W. *Modern systems research for the behavioral scientist.* Chicago: Aldine, 1968.

Cherns, A. B. "The principles of sociotechnical design." *Human Relations 29* (1976):783–792.

Cummings, T. G., and S. Srivastva. *Management of work: A socio-technical systems approach.* Kent, Ohio: Kent State Press, 1977.

Davis, L. E., and A. B. Cherns. *The quality of working life.* Vols. I and II. New York: Free Press, 1975.

Davis, L. E., and J. C. Taylor. *Design of jobs.* 2nd ed. Santa Monica, Calif.: Goodyear, 1979.

Deal, T. E., and A. A. Kennedy. *Corporate cultures.* Reading, Mass.: Addison-Wesley, 1982.

Deming, W. E. *Quality, productivity, and competitive position.* Cambridge, Mass.: MIT, 1982.

Drucker, P. F. "Business purpose and mission." In *Management: Tasks, responsibilities, practices.* New York: Harper & Row, 1974. 74–94.

Dyer, W. G., and W. G. Dyer, Jr. "Organization development: System change or culture change?" *Personnel* (February 1986):14–22.

Elliott, O. "Beyond sociotechnical/open system design." Paper presented at the forty-fifth National Academy of Management Conference, Boston, Mass., 1984.

Elliott, O., A. B. Shani, and D. P. Hanna. "Strategic thinking and sociotechnical system design: A high tech merger." Paper presented at the 26th Annual Conference of the Western Academy of Management, San Diego, Calif., 1985.

Elliott, O., and A. B. Shani. "Strategy and organization design dynamics: A high-tech case study." *The emerging practice of OD: four decades old and growing.* NTL/University Associates, to be published in 1988.

Emery, F. E., ed. *Systems thinking.* Baltimore: Penguin, 1969.

Emery, F. E., and E. L. Trist. "Socio-technical systems." In Churchman, C. W. and M. Verhuist, eds., *Management sciences models and techniques.* Vol. 2. London: Pergamon Press, 1960.

Emery, F. E., and E. L. Trist. "Analytical model for sociotechnical systems." In Pasmore, W. A., and J. J. Sherwood, eds., *Sociotechnical systems: A sourcebook,* 120–131. La Jolla, Calif.: University Associates, 1978.

Galbraith, J. R. *Organization design.* Reading, Mass.: Addison-Wesley, 1977.

Galbraith, J. R., and D. A. Nathanson. *Strategy implementation: The role of structure and process.* St. Paul, Minn.: West, 1978.

Gyllenhammar, P. G. *People at work.* Reading, Mass.: Addison-Wesley, 1977.

Gyllenhammar, P. G. "How Volvo adapts work to people." *Harvard Business Review* (July-August, 1977):102–113.

Hackman, J. R., and G. R. Oldham. *Work redesign.* Reading, Mass.: Addison-Wesley, 1980.

Hackman, J. R., and J. L. Suttle, eds. *Improving life at work: Behavioral science approaches to organizational change.* Santa Monica, Calif.: Goodyear, 1977.

Handy, C. B. *Understanding organizations.* New York: Penguin, 1981.

Harrison, R. "Understanding your organization's character." In Jones, J. E., and J. W. Pfeiffer, eds., *The 1975 annual handbook for group facilitators,* 199–209. La Jolla, Calif.: University Associates, 1975.

Harrison, R. "Understanding your organization's culture." Unpublished manuscript, 1986.

Herbst, P. G. *Socio-technical design: Strategies in multidisciplinary research.* London: Tavistock, 1974.

Herzberg, F. *Work and the nature of man.* Cleveland: World, 1966.

Herzberg, F. "One more time: How do you motivate employees?" *Harvard Business Review* (January-February 1968):53–62.

Hill, P. *Towards a new philosophy of management* (revised reprint). Epping, Essex, Great Britain: Gower Press, 1976.

Kanter, R. M. *The change masters: Innovation for productivity in the American corporation.* New York: Simon & Schuster, 1983.

Kast, F. E., and J. E. Rosenzweig. *Organization and management: A systems approach.* 2nd ed., 137–141. New York: McGraw-Hill, 1974.

Katz, D., and R. L. Kahn. *The social psychology of organizations.* 2nd ed. New York: Wiley, 1978.

Kilmann, R. H. *Beyond the quick fix.* San Francisco: Jossey-Bass, 1984.

Kotter, J. P., L. A. Schlesinger, and V. Sathe. *Organization: Text, cases, and readings on the management of organizational design and change.* 2nd ed. Homewood, Ill.: Irwin, 1986.

Krone, Charles. Open systems redesign. In Burke, W. W., ed., *New technologies in organization development: II*. La Jolla, Calif.: University Associates, 1974.

Lawler, E. E., III. "The new plant revolution." *Organizational Dynamics* (Winter 1978):2–12.

Lawler, E. E., III. *Motivation in work organizations*. Monterey, Calif.: Brooks/Cole, 1973.

Lawrence, P. R., and J. W. Lorsch. *Organization and environment*. Boston: Harvard Press, 1967.

MacMillan, I. C., and P. E. Jones. "Designing organizations to compete." *The Journal of Business Strategy* (Spring 1984):11–26.

Miller, E. J. "Technology, territory, and time: The internal differentiation of complex production systems." In Pasmore, W. A., and J. J. Sherwood, eds., *Sociotechnical systems: A sourcebook*, 96–119. La Jolla, Calif.: University Associates, 1978.

Miller, J. G. *Living systems*. New York: McGraw-Hill, 1978.

Morgan, G. *Images of organization*. Beverly Hills, Calif.: Sage, 1986.

Nadler, D. A. *Feedback and organization development: Using data-based methods*. Reading, Mass.: Addison-Wesley, 1977.

Nadler, D. A., and M. L. Tushman. "A model for diagnosing organizational behavior." *Organizational Dynamics* (Autumn 1980): 35–51.

Nadler, D. A., and M. L. Tushman. *Concepts for the design of organizations*. New York: OR&C Inc., 1982.

Pasmore, W. A., and J. J. Sherwood, eds. *Sociotechnical systems: A sourcebook*. La Jolla, Calif.: University Associates, 1978.

Pava, C. *Managing new office technology — An organizational strategy*. New York: Free Press, 1983.

Peters, T. J., and R. H. Waterman, Jr. *In search of excellence*. New York: Harper & Row, 1982.

Schein, E. H. *Organizational culture and leadership*. San Francisco: Jossey-Bass, 1985.

Sherwood, J. J. "Creating work cultures with competitive advantage." Unpublished paper, 1987.

Srivastva, S., P. F. Salipante, Jr., T. G. Cummings, W. W. Notz, J. D. Bigelow, and J. A. Waters. *Job satisfaction and productivity.* Kent, Ohio: The Comparative Administration Research Institute, Kent State University Press, 1977.

Taylor, F. W. *The principles of scientific management.* New York: Harper, 1911.

Taylor, J. C. "The human side of work: The socio-technical approach to work system design." *Personnel Review* (Summer 1975):17–22.

Taylor, T. O., D. J. Friedman, and D. Couture. "Operating without supervisors: An experiment." *Organizational Dynamics* (Winter 1987):26–38.

Tichy, N. M., and J. N. Nisberg. "When does work restructuring work? Organizational innovations at Volvo and GM." *Organizational Dynamics* (Summer 1976):63–80.

Thomas, R. R., Jr. "Guidelines for identifying organizational culture." Unpublished paper, 1983.

Thompson, J. D. *Organizations in action.* New York: McGraw-Hill, 1967.

Trist, E. L. "The evolution of socio-technical systems: A conceptual framework and an action research program." Ontario Quality of Working Life Centre, Issues in the Quality of Working Life Occasional Paper Number 2, June 1981.

Trist, E. L., and K. W. Bamforth. "Some social and psychological consequences of the long-wall method of coal-getting." *Human Relations* 4:3–38.

Vail, P. B. "The purposing of high-performing systems." *Organizational Dynamics* (Autumn 1982):23–39.

von Bertalanffy, L. "The theory of open systems in physics and biology." *Science* 111(1950):23–28.

von Bertalanffy, L. "General system theory." *General Systems.* Yearbook of the Society for the Advancement of General System Theory 1(1956):1–10.

Walton, R. E. "How to counter alienation in the plant." *Harvard Business Review, 50* (November-December 1972):70–81.

Walton, R. E. "From Hawthorne to Topeka and Kalmar." In E. L. Cass

and F. G. Zimmer, eds., *Man and work in society*. New York: Van Nostrand Reinhold, 1975.

Walton, R. E. "The diffusion of new work structures: Explaining why success didn't take." *Organizational Dynamics* (Winter 1975): 3–22.

Walton, R. E. "Successful strategies for diffusing work innovations." *Journal of Contemporary Business* 6(1977):1–22.

Walton, R. E., and L. S. Schlesinger. "Do supervisors thrive in participative work systems?" *Organizational Dynamics* (Winter 1979): 24–38.

Waterman, R. H., Jr. "Structure is not organization." McKinsey Staff Paper, 1979.

Weber, M. *The theory of social and economic organization* (translated by Henderson, A. M. and Parsons, T.). Parsons, T., ed. New York: Free Press, 1947.

Weick, K. E. *The social psychology of organizing*. 2nd ed. Reading, Mass.: Addison-Wesley, 1979.

Weick, K. E. "Organization design: Organizations as self-designing systems." *Organizational Dynamics* (Autumn 1977):31–46.

Weisbord, M. R. "The two first laws of diagnosis and action." Unpublished paper.

Weisbord, M. R. *Organizational diagnosis: A workbook of theory and practice*. Reading, Mass.: Addison-Wesley, 1977.

Wilkins, A. L. "The culture audit: A tool for understanding organizations." *Organizational Dynamics* (Autumn 1983):24–38.